RECOGNITION REDEFINED

Building Self-Esteem at Work

Roger L. Hale

Rita F. Maehling

MONOCHROME
Press ꩜

Subsidiary of Gray Media, Inc.
Exeter, New Hampshire

© 1993 by Monochrome Press, Inc.

All rights reserved. This book or parts thereof may not be reproduced in any form without permission of the publisher.

ISBN: 1-882407-04-0

Library of Congress Catalog Card Number: 93-78777

Manufactured in the United States of America by
Maple-Vail Book Manufacturing Group

10 9 8 7 6 5 4 3 2 1

First published in 1992 by Tennant Company, Minneapolis, Minnesota
Bonnie Anderson, Project Director
Susan Mundale, Managing Editor
Mame Osteen, Contributing Writer
Rachel Fine, Graphic Designer
Jackie Urbanovic, Illustrator
Rita Maehling, Co-Author and Project Manager
Denise Parks, Contributing Editor
Richard Radomsky, Contributing Editor

Dedication

This book, like *Quest for Quality*, is dedicated to the many generations of Tennant employees, at all levels of the company, who have truly believed in people as the foundation of a good enterprise. This belief has formed the culture in which a quality emphasis — and consequently recognition — could take root and grow.

Table of Contents

Introduction

American business is being battered with questions about competitiveness, productivity, and even survival. How are we going to compete with the sophisticated technologies of Germany and Japan, and the eager labor force of emerging nations at the same time? After we downsize and restructure, how do we produce better products with fewer people and leaner resources? As competition for skilled employees heightens, how can we attract the right people, and keep them working at their best?

At Tennant, we saw these questions on the horizon more than a decade ago when we began exploring the concept of quality. We had excellent products respected for quality at home and abroad. But we knew that we couldn't be complacent. We set out to maintain and improve our stature in the world of floor maintenance products.

In 1979, we invited Phil Crosby to work with us, and we used his book *Quality is Free* as our primer. In *Quality is Free*, Crosby listed 14 steps to total quality improvement. Step 12 is recognition, and he devoted two pages of this 270-page book to why recognition is important. However, he didn't give specific directions for making recognition part of a quality process. That we had to learn on our own.

We found that most companies did little to recognize high performers beyond promotions, salary increases, and bonuses. And although the behaviorists — primarily Maslow, Herzberg, and Skinner — had explored the effects of positive reinforcement and rewards on performance, little had been done to apply their findings to the world of work.

We began by defining an objective — to recognize superior quality performers — and putting in place an annual program to recognize individuals and teams for their efforts. Our intent was to identify role models who exemplified outstanding efforts toward quality improvement. Once the program was in place, we listened to employees' reactions. It became clear that recognizing a few people once a year wasn't going to make a difference. People needed to know on a regular basis that what they did was appreciated. And some employees wondered if choosing a few "winners" every year made the rest of them "losers." We had many people making excellent contributions. We needed to recognize more people, more often.

We also realized that the same type of recognition doesn't work for everyone. We learned that successful recognition needs three dimensions: formal, informal, and day-to-day ways to recognize people for their contributions.

Over the years, developing self-esteem has become the philosophical core of recognition at Tennant. Self-esteem helps us maintain our mental health and stay centered in the ever-changing environment of work. If we don't feel good about the work we're doing, no wonder so many of us look to other stimuli to satisfy us.

But rewarding and recognizing employees isn't easy. As organizations flatten their hierarchical structures, promotions become less and less available as a reward for high performance, and pay increases can't always be given. So how do we let employees know we value their contributions?

We believe that regular, structured recognition plays a key role in increasing self-esteem. And we believe that the three-dimensional approach is key. Like a three-legged stool, each dimension plays a critical role. Take away one leg of the stool, and it falls.

We wrote this book to bring together what we have learned about recognition over the past decade. Many of the ideas are not new. But we have put them to work, and they have become part of our culture. Now we want to share our experience with you.

This book isn't only about Tennant's recognition experiences, however. During the past few years, we've interacted with hundreds of other organizations, in both the private and the public sectors, who are also grappling with recognition. We'll tell you some of their stories as well as our own as this book unfolds.

We don't claim to have all the answers to the questions that American business faces. We do know that recognition has made a difference in the quality of Tennant's products, and in the enthusiasm, dedication, and commitment of the people who make up our company. For us, recognition is a part of our corporate culture. We hope that in this book you find inspiration and practical advice for making it a part of yours as well.

Roger L. Hale
Rita F. Maehling
July 1992

People who feel good about themselves produce good results.

Chapter 1

The Tennant Company Experience

We all like to feel good about ourselves. And we **need** to feel that way if we're going to be happy, productive members of society. To have our contributions recognized and our personal values reinforced sustains us and helps us grow.

Nowhere is this simple truth more dramatically demonstrated than in the workplace. Employees who are encouraged to contribute to the efficiency and productivity of their organization, and are then recognized for their efforts, will be more motivated and more productive. And recognition is the key.

Though the concept of employee recognition is simple, it is difficult to implement. In practice, employee recognition is a multidimensional process demanding varied and numerous skills, which must be learned and applied.

In 1979, Tennant made a commitment to "do it right the first time" by initiating a quality improvement process. Since then, the road to employee recognition — an integral part of the process — has been an enormous challenge. After 13 years of trial and error, persistence, and hard work, we'd like to say we've finally got it right. And in some ways that's true. We know what to do. But providing exemplary recognition is an ongoing effort, as you'll see.

Let's go back to the beginning of our journey to see how Tennant first learned about the vital importance of employee recognition.

QUALITY CONSCIOUSNESS COMES TO TENNANT

In the late 1970s, American businesses were in the midst of an identity crisis. Long regarded as the industrial leaders of the world, American companies faced a new global market and increased competition that left them grappling with new standards of performance and quality. A corporation's ability to achieve consistent and superior quality performance was fast becoming essential, not just to succeed but to survive.

At Tennant we began to examine our quality standards in 1979. At the time, we had little reason to doubt our ability to compete. We were winners. Tennant was more than a century old and well-established as one of the world's leading manufacturers of industrial and commercial floor coatings, sweepers, scrubbers, and scarifiers.

Our company had survived the recession of 1973-75, with its spiraling inflation and oil embargo. But we had also witnessed Japan's growing dominance in the automobile and electronics markets and its outstanding achievements in productivity, quality, and reliability. Obviously, the Japanese were on to something.

At Tennant, we decided to take a closer look at our own systems and processes and to improve them wherever possible. But how? We found the answer to that in a book by Philip B. Crosby, *Quality is Free.*[1]

Using Crosby's 14-step approach, we tackled the areas of problem solving, cost reduction, and quality improvement. Working directly with Crosby one day a month for the first year, we began to systematically apply his methods to every area of our company. The process was enlightening. It led to a new definition of quality for Tennant.

We came to see that quality means identifying the requirements of the job, finding ways to measure them, and meeting those requirements by doing things right the first time.

To demonstrate our commitment to the process, we developed a policy statement, signed by our President Roger Hale. Then we shared the pledge with our employees to involve them in Tennant's new commitment to quality.

AMBITIONS BLOOM

The quality improvement process that began to unfold later that year was led by management. Executives laid the groundwork with the first quality process plans. Middle managers and hourly employees and supervisors from all across the company were involved in an initial pilot program to reduce defects and improve efficiency — that was our first Quality Team. Their ambitious goals included establishing quality management in every operation, eliminating nonconformances, and reducing the ultimate cost of quality.

Although our employees were informed of these goals and changes during the early stages of the process, the programs really blossomed when the company began to communicate openly with employees, involving them in making the new system work, and recognizing them for their efforts. The combination of those actions — heightened communication, increased involvement, and then recognition for employee progress and achievements — gave everyone a sense of common purpose. In essence, it said, "We want your ideas and we need your help to succeed." Bringing employees into the process gave them a special vote of confidence and boosted their self-esteem. As time went by, we began to discover the role employee self-esteem plays in a successful organization.

MEETING CHALLENGES

Self-esteem is a fundamental part of human emotion. Though psychologists differ, they generally define self-esteem as the self-confidence that allows a person to meet the challenges of life. Regardless of its definition, we do know that self-esteem comes from within. Says Ken Blanchard, co-author of *The One Minute Manager,* "Self-esteem is like a door that is locked from the inside."[2] Behind that door, we evaluate ourselves as human beings. The internal dialogues we engage in after our successes and failures make a difference in whether we fail or succeed in the future. Psychologist Nathaniel Branden says, "Self-esteem is the reputation we acquire with ourselves."[3] Self-esteem dictates our success in life, both at home and on the job.

> *"The greatest barrier to achievement and success is not lack of talent or ability, but lack of self-esteem."*
>
> **Dr. Nathaniel Branden**
> **Psychologist**

A person with high self-esteem possesses self-confidence and self-respect. A strong sense of self-worth helps a person meet difficult challenges and demanding goals. A general sense of empowerment and being in control encourages a person to seek out the difficult and demanding. Setbacks or failures are not perceived as evidence of unworthiness; they inspire perseverance. Guided by an internal strength, the person with high self-esteem chooses his or her own path and follows it, knowing that he or she can make a difference.

On the other hand, people with low self-esteem are plagued with feelings of inadequacy. To cope, they seek refuge and safety in familiar and undemanding circumstances. Achievement and success above a certain level are outside their self-concept (their internal image of who they are) and what they believe is appropriate for them. Guided by these negative inner beliefs, people with low self-esteem set their sights low. They stay in the background, don't contribute, compete, improve, or succeed, especially in their own estimation. They are their own worst enemies.

SELF-ESTEEM AND WORK

The essence of work is performance. How employees perceive their own performance on the job affects their self-esteem. From management's perspective, high self-esteem is a valuable employee asset. "Workers with high self-esteem are more productive, autonomous, responsible, and creative; they are less angry at the boss and less often absent," says John Vasconcellos, a 24-year veteran of the California Legislature and leader of the state's task force studying the sociological, psychological, and economic aspects of self-esteem.[4]

Here are two examples of self-esteem at work:

Each day Kathy begins work as an administrative assistant for ABC Corporation. Today, as usual, she arrives at 8:55 but stops to talk with another employee until 9:05 a.m. Her day is slow and predictable. Throughout the day she does what is asked of her but not much else. If the phone rings near her break or lunch hour, she ignores it because she doesn't want it to interfere with "her time." Later in the day she submits a report to her boss. She could have done better, but she knows her boss will accept it. As 5 p.m. approaches, she starts watching the clock and avoids beginning a project that might run later. At 5 p.m. she's out the door.

Across town, Judy, an administrative assistant for XYZ Corporation, is busily at work on a report her boss needs by the end of the week. The subject of the report is fascinating, and she volunteered to write it so she could learn more about the company's operation. She did extra research to improve it and she realizes she'll have to come in early tomorrow to finish it up. But that's OK. At 5:50 she takes a phone call, though the office has been closed for nearly an hour. By the time she's ready to leave the office, the night security guard is on duty.

Kathy and Judy have similar abilities, but their performances are vastly different. The reasons for the disparity in performance can be understood if we look at their respective levels of self-esteem.

Kathy, plagued with low self-esteem, creates an atmosphere of dull routine. Lulled into a feeling of safety by the monotony of defined tasks, she tries to become invisible. She ventures nothing and gains nothing. She tries to avoid failure, but she is actually avoiding success. Afraid to draw negative attention to herself, she tends to get by with as little effort as possible. Her job is a refuge, not an opportunity.

"People want recognition. People will sometimes work very conscientiously in terrible environments, if they get the proper recognition. The facilities won't win them over. You've got to win their commitment to the job—but you can't buy good performance with just money."

Adapted from "Recognition Vital to Keeping Workers Content," Distribution Center Management, Vol. 24, No. 1, January 1989

Judy learns everything she can about her job. She expands her knowledge, constantly searching for more effective ways to complete her tasks. Judy has high self-esteem and creates her own success. She performs well, which nurtures her feelings of self-esteem. As her self-esteem increases, so does her capacity to perform better. She begins to occupy a sphere of control and recognizes that her actions have value. She then stretches her boundaries by broadening her range of actions, taking initiative, and risking involvement.

Using these examples, it seems evident that an individual's performance at work mirrors that person's level of self-esteem. So, if you're going to hire someone, you probably should hire an applicant with high self-esteem. Then you'll never have a problem employee, someone who fails to work to full potential.

Unfortunately, it's not that simple. Self-esteem is not fixed. Self-esteem changes, day to day, even hour to hour. Managers can't **make** people feel good about themselves, but managers can create a work environment that invites people to feel good about themselves and their work. Improving employee self-esteem through recognition is an important goal for every manager.

RECOGNIZING RECOGNITION

Everyone needs recognition. It helps people measure their performance. We all want to perform well. But we're only certain we've done so when other people tell us. Some people can perform at a high level with no recognition. But even the most confident, self-motivated people eventually feel taken for granted without an occasional positive comment or pat on the back. They may get the impression that we do not value their work. If so, they might look for another job. If they stay on, their performance will probably decline. Given recognition however, their performance will remain high and boost the self-esteem of others. According to performance management consultant Janis Allen, recognition is a powerful tool for reinforcing specific behaviors.[5] Self-motivation, the ability to perform on one's own, is not innate — it is learned. The same is true for other performance characteristics, including determination, assertiveness, and pride in a job well done.

When a manager compliments an employee on his or her planning, attention to detail, and follow-up, the manager is making the employee aware of specific, desirable behaviors. Every time the employee repeats that behavior, he or she recalls the recognition received from the manager. The next time the employee is faced with a similar project, he or she will be much more likely to repeat that reinforced behavior.

8

ENHANCING THE WORK LIFE OF EMPLOYEES

Step 11 in Phil Crosby's 14-step program suggests that organizations encourage employees to let management know what obstacles prevent them from improving quality. Tennant started to do that in 1980 and was amazed by the results.

> *"One of the greatest opportunities that comes from the quality program is the chance for someone like me, who works hard with his hands, to work with his head by making decisions. It makes me feel good, it makes me feel important."*
>
> **Leo Fautsch,
> Tennant**

In the first six months, we received 1,200 responses from employees identifying specific problems. This information avalanche taught us a lesson: We realized that we had to bring into the process the people who were doing the work.

That year, in a visit to Tennant by a group of Japanese managers, their leader made a brief speech to our managers and supervisors. He said that the quality effort had been successful in Japan because it allowed workers to have some control over their jobs. He emphasized that the purpose of a quality effort was not only to create defect-free products but also to enhance the work life of employees. He told us that participation, cooperation, and teamwork bring out the best in employees. Their involvement enhances their job satisfaction and their self-esteem. Ultimately it improves the organization's efficiency and productivity.

This simple concept stripped away our long-held assumptions about business organization and management and allowed us to see Tennant in a new perspective. It was one of our first lessons: To achieve our quality goal, we had to meet the needs of our employees. And we believed that recognition was one of those needs.

9

LEARNING THE ROPES

When Tennant began developing a recognition program in 1980-81, we decided that one of our goals would be to recognize superior quality performers, both individuals and teams. In this way, we would create role models for others to follow as we worked toward quality improvement.

Though our goal was quality, we were really setting in motion a complete behavioral change for the entire company. No simple task.

To recognize our quality performers we created a formal awards program for groups and individuals. (More about this in Chapter 5.)

Once a year for individuals and twice a year for groups, this formal program recognized some of Tennant's outstanding per-formers. When we asked employees for feedback on the program, however, one message came through loud and clear — it wasn't enough. The awards program provided well-deserved recognition to a few Tennant employees, but didn't recognize enough people often enough.

RETURN TO THE QUALITY MODEL

Employees were telling us we needed broader forms of recognition used much more often. Crosby's 12th step told us to provide recognition, but didn't tell us how. So we reassessed our quality process. We saw that when we first began to strive toward improved product quality, we defined quality as "conforming to requirements."

Now we had to define recognition by applying the same model. In this case we were determining the requirements of Tennant employees, employees we wanted to recognize. Now we had to identify their requirements for recognition and satisfaction.

Our discoveries are described in the following chapters of this book. Many answers came from Tennant employees; others were picked up from psychologists, behaviorists, and performance managers; still others from companies that worked with us to develop their own recognition programs.

Before we move on, we will briefly review the recognition program we've built at Tennant.

THE THREE-DIMENSIONAL MODEL

Today we know that recognition is not a "one-size-fits-all" concept. People are different and so are their needs for recognition.

Some differences are strictly a matter of personal preference. Others are linked to an employee's age or career status. Our goal has been to understand and meet the diverse needs of employees with a variety of recognition techniques.

To help visualize our recognition program, we use the idea of a three-legged stool: Formal recognition, informal recognition, and day-to-day recognition are the three legs that form the solid footing of our employee recognition program. With only one type of recognition, or even two, the stool topples over. All three types, working together, are necessary for a viable program.

ACHIEVING QUALITY RECOGNITION

Creating and improving our recognition program is an intensive quality process all its own. In *Quest for Quality*, we recount our quality improvement efforts, citing the five "Key Elements of Success" we felt were necessary to achieve lasting quality improvement:

1. Management commitment
2. Employee involvement

3. Worker/manager relationships that are cooperative, not adversarial
4. Rewards for the people
5. Time, energy, and determination

That fourth concept, "Rewards for the people," focuses specifically on the need for employee recognition. And we can now see that recognition is actually a microcosm of the entire quality process. The same elements that contribute to the success of our quality efforts are essential to the development of a successful recognition system.

MANAGEMENT COMMITMENT

Our commitment to recognition, like our commitment to quality, requires the full backing of management at all levels. That translates into time, money, and personal involvement.

At Tennant, commitment to recognition comes from the top. Once a self-proclaimed skeptic, President Roger Hale has become a champion of recognition. In his early efforts to understand the concept, he studied the psychological and sociological aspects of the subject. In the process, he became an advocate, uncovering information that is used in our recognition training today.

Roger has also changed his own behavior, using reinforcement and recognition techniques on a regular basis. He often writes personal notes of praise and encouragement to those involved in the recognition process. He enjoys acknowledging an individual's contribution on a special project with the person's peers. He also reinforces the importance of the recognition process in his President's Column in *TENNANT TOPICS*, our employee newsletter.

In addition, management's commitment to recognition is demonstrated through the company's sustained efforts to increase recognition awareness and skills. In 1981, Tennant introduced the formal recognition concept to managers, setting down the program's goals and enlisting their support. Later, when we began to understand the complexity and the skills required for a successful informal recognition program, we boosted our efforts. In 1984, we introduced managers to the positive feedback skills necessary for day-to-day recognition. And in 1989, Tennant created a Quality Services Department, composed of four people with a two-part mission. The focus of the internal mission is to help our employees improve and sustain their quality efforts. The second part is to market components of Tennant's Customer-Focused Quality Process.

> *"Employees work for pay, but they're looking for a chance to help govern the business and to do a better quality job. They also want recognition for extraordinary achievement."*
>
> **Total Quality at Chrysler, Commitment Plus, Vol. 5, No. 12, October 1990**

In 1990, all of Tennant's 245 managers, supervisors, and lead people took a four-hour seminar, which is based on the three-dimensional recognition model and designed to heighten awareness of the importance of recognition and emphasize the need for day-to-day recognition and positive feedback.

To further reinforce management commitment to our recognition efforts, we included demonstration of recognition skills and participation in the program as part of the performance reviews for our managers, supervisors, and all employees.

The recognition process is still evolving and will probably continue to do so. Skills must be practiced and refined, and our company is committed to employee recognition and demonstrates that commitment in our plans and actions at every management level.

EMPLOYEE INVOLVEMENT

"Prior to our quality improvement process, we hired people to do their jobs and nothing else," said Roger Hale. "We didn't ask production employees to help design new products or improve procedures. But the quality emphasis allowed us to tap the knowledge and skill of our production workers. We could ask them to become involved to help us achieve our goals."[6] Roger's statement is typical of the new attitude at Tennant.

The entire process of employee involvement is like a perpetual motion machine. Employee involvement requires increased communication between managers and employees. With increased communication comes greater understanding. Barriers break down and cooperation improves. As our Japanese visitor said in 1980, the whole process contributes to employee empowerment, satisfaction, and self-esteem. Enhanced self-esteem leads to increased productivity. And on it goes.

"We feel the greatest potential obstacle to future progress in the Quality Process will be ineffective managers," the first Quality Team report stated in 1982. The report cited the following management behaviors that needed to be modified and improved to achieve Tennant's quality goals:

1. Managers who didn't know how to get their people involved in problem solving and decision making.
2. Managers who didn't know how to develop their people into highly skilled workers and leaders.
3. Managers who didn't know how to teach by example.
4. Managers who didn't know how to develop an organizational climate to foster high performance.
5. Managers who didn't know how to listen.

Tennant's managers were doing the jobs they were taught to do. But the jobs had changed. The management techniques that had worked for decades were no longer viable. Our new quality effort called for new behaviors, not only on the production line but also at the management level. Our managers were eager to support the quality effort, but as the report cited, they "didn't know how."

We soon began an intensive training program to teach them how to increase their awareness and give them new behavioral techniques.

"The ability to listen to each other carefully and respectfully was essential to our recognition goals," says Quality Services Manager Rita Maehling. With the help of Unisys Corporation, Tennant created a training program designed to improve employee listening skills. The course, mandatory for Tennant's then 1,500 employees, was completed in 1983-84.

In the 1990s, effective listening is being widely recognized as an essential management skill. "Listening helps people feel understood and supported, which in turn helps them do better work," says Ken Blanchard. "In addition, good listening skills strengthen relationships between managers and employees by creating mutual respect."[7]

Along with listening, Tennant tackled another problem area with training programs designed to teach employees how to work effectively in groups and teams.[8] Through these courses, barriers separating managers from employees or one department from another began to disappear.

> *"If management is to help create a climate conducive to high quality, its emphasis should be on high standards, respect for the individual, effective communication, and a reward and recognition process that benefits the producers."*
>
> **John M. Davis,
> Tennant**

COOPERATIVE/ NONADVERSARIAL RELATIONSHIPS

When recently asked how he would revise and update *The One Minute Manager* for the 1990s, Ken Blanchard said that enhancing employee self-esteem and improving communication skills would now be crucial points in the book. "People who feel good about themselves produce good results," said Blanchard. "Managers must communicate genuine respect and concern to their employees by helping them enhance their self-image and feel better about themselves and their performance."[9]

To accomplish this goal, managers must develop a cooperative and nonadversarial atmosphere at work. Without ongoing positive interactions between people, any attempt at meaningful recognition appears insincere or gimmicky. It's simply not possible.

> *"If you recognize people for their jobs, they're going to try harder and feel better about themselves."*
>
> **Tennant Award of Excellence Recipient**

A cooperative, nonadversarial attitude, however, does not mean managers have to lower their high standards of performance. On the contrary, managers have a responsibility to let employees know what exactly is expected of them. Telling the employee what you want is not adversarial — it is a positive exchange of information. When employees know the company's standards and guidelines, they know what behaviors are required to do the job well. When a manager supports that effort through positive feedback, the employee feels good about it. It's a constant, cyclical, give-and-take system.

"Changing human behavior requires skills that many people lack but everyone can learn," reported *Quality Progress* magazine[10] in June 1991. That is the essence of the Tennant philosophy. Ongoing communication with employees and frequent skills-training seminars are helping us continually fine-tune our cooperative, nonadversarial working relationships. We'll talk more about this in Chapter 7.

TIME, ENERGY, AND DETERMINATION

Tennant's goal to master the art of employee recognition is long term. At Tennant, our recognition efforts have been evolving for more than 12 years, and we are still in the process of change. But we have seen results: behaviors have changed, job satisfaction has improved; we have increased communication and interaction, and have seen a growing enthusiasm for our recognition efforts. What began as a simple, one-dimensional program has now become an integral part of our culture. Knowledge and awareness of the role of recognition have changed the way we see ourselves at Tennant.

No program of such magnitude can be achieved without dedication, effort, patience, and perseverance. But the results are well worth the effort.

THE FUTURE OF AMERICAN BUSINESS

As we look to the future, we must consider the impact that current economic and social trends are having on business structure and organization.

The corporate belt-tightening of the 1980s, brought on by world market changes, has led to a flattening of the management hierarchy in many large corporations. According to management trend analyst John Zenger, president of Zenger-Miller of San Jose, California, one-third of all middle managers in Fortune 500 companies have been removed and will not be replaced.[11] While some of these changes are the result of economics, the new "lean and mean" corporate structure reflects the same discoveries we made

at Tennant when we implemented our quality program —
empowered employees can make many decisions for themselves.

For those middle managers that remain and those employees
seeking to move up through the ranks, the diminishing expecta-
tion of promotion is compounded by another pivotal factor. The
famous "Baby Boom" generation, now in its 30s and 40s, is creating a conspicuous bulge in company ranks nationwide. These
Baby Boomers, most of them well-established in their careers and
prepared for the climb, must compete with a larger number of
candidates for a dwindling number of positions.

That being the case, what are the alternatives to continued
promotion? How can we show employees that their contributions
are valued and that they are important members of the company?
We believe that recognition can help fill the need by building
employee self-esteem, which leads to increased job satisfaction.

In 1987, according to the American Productivity and Quality
Center, 91 percent of all employees value recognition for a job
well done. Yet only half say they get that recognition.[12] So we have
a long way to go.

The welders' creative problem solving made giant gains in helping Tennant improve the big picture.

Chapter 2

Benefits of Recognition

After Tennant began its recognition journey, everyone involved soon realized that recognition is a process, not merely a program. Along the way, we changed, adapted, and ultimately developed new perspectives on employee communication, involvement, and action that have permeated every level of our company. At Tennant today, recognition is not just a peripheral system of goals and rewards, but an integral part of our corporate culture. By constantly striving to meet the needs of all employees, we've come to realize far-reaching benefits from our recognition philosophy.

WHY RECOGNIZING RESULTS DOESN'T WORK

Recognition exists in some form in many American companies. But it is usually narrowly defined and used most often to identify results that benefit the company. Janis Allen, a performance management consultant and co-author of *I Saw What You Did & I Know Who You Are: Giving & Receiving Recognition,* says that even today recognition is often tied only to the **results** of the employee's efforts, not to his or her contributions to those results. At Tennant, we believe the results-oriented approach renders recognition not only less effective but perhaps destructive to employee morale.

For example, if a manager says, "Congratulations, our sales are up this month," he or she is focusing on the benefits to the company. The individual's contribution is not being recognized.

Of course, people produce the company's results, and people need recognition. Instead of saying, "Our sales are up this month," it is much more meaningful to say, "Jane, you've increased your prospecting by 15 percent for the last three months, and it's boosted our sales. Great job!"

Recognition of individuals and groups is uplifting and encouraging because it tells the employee what he or she did that was worthy of praise.

THE TRADITIONS OF RECOGNITION

Rewards and recognition have long been the hallmark of many sales organizations. Sales bring in revenues which directly affect the bottom line. Sales are easily quantifiable. Sales representatives have quotas to meet. Reaching or exceeding those quotas is a measure of success, which is rewarded at annual recognition banquets or with company-sponsored trips and prizes.

This approach overlooks the majority of a company's workers: assembly line workers who build or produce the product, the administrative staff that supports the company, the customer service representatives who deal directly with the public. They all contribute to the company's success, but their efforts are more difficult to measure. As a result, significant opportunities to improve quality and increase productivity in design, production, inventory, administration, customer service — all of which affect the bottom line — are often neglected by the majority of American corporations.

COST OF QUALITY

Tennant was part of that majority until Phil Crosby introduced us to the "zero defects" concept. He broadened our vision of Tennant's mission and expanded our opportunities to achieve excellence. When we were challenged to "do it right the first time," we realized that everyone at Tennant had something to contribute to the quality process. We were challenged to maximize employee motivation and participation across the company. We had to create a way to give everyone a stake in our vision for the future by putting "something in it for the people." This was a radical departure from the way many companies still do business.

HIERARCHY AND THE NEW AMERICAN WORKER

In a 1992 *Wall Street Journal* article, University of Pennsylvania technology historian Thomas Hughes said most U.S. industrial companies still follow the "scientific management" precepts outlined in the 1920s, which prescribed static roles for everyone in the organization.[1] Managers were paid to think. Workers, who in the 1920s consisted largely of immigrants or recent migrants from rural areas, were paid to follow orders. This structured hierarchy worked well, and the United States soon joined the ranks of the world's major industrial powers.

The "scientific management" doctrine was later fortified by World War II military-management techniques, which were also hierarchical but included strict confidentiality to avoid information leaks. Like foot soldiers, employees of the 1940s and 1950s were told only what was necessary to accomplish a particular task, and no more. Secrecy, or closely held information, created a barrier between the elite group that was "in the know" and the vast majority of employees outside the inner circle.

At Tennant, we came to believe that this antiquated management structure stifles and inhibits employee productivity, erodes job satisfaction, and makes a genuine and effective recognition program impossible.

The old management system doesn't work anymore because more than half a century of dramatic social change has altered the American worker.

No longer a group of newly arrived immigrants and uneducated rural folk, today's American work force consists of literate, skilled, independent-minded workers. Many of them are Baby Boomers, predominantly well-educated and well-informed, who, when they joined the work force, didn't particularly like the American business hierarchy, and had greater expectations of their jobs than workers of the past. Judith M. Bardwick, a management consultant on the Baby Boom generation, says, "Boomers at all levels want to be valued as integral members of the organization — not just cogs in a wheel."[2]

> *"Organizations that get high service marks from their customers are likely to have a systematic way of telling employees they're important. Managers know that the celebration of organizational, group, and individual service accomplishment is essential if the delivery of high quality service is to be the norm, not the exception."*
>
> **Ron Zemke**
> **Performance Research**
> **Associates**

Another element of the work force, the Baby Bust generation, are those Americans born after 1964 who began to enter the working ranks in the last decade. What sets the "Busters" apart from their predecessors is not their lack of respect for traditional management hierarchy or their increased self-reliance, but their sense of entitlement. Unlike Baby Boomers, Baby Busters don't expect to pay their dues before earning the right to participate. They expect to participate now and to be kept informed — on what is expected of them, and what they can expect in return.

Though Baby Boomers and Busters exhibit differences in style, they share many of the same values regarding work. In a 1989 national study of 1,001 American workers, ages 25-49, nearly 75 percent said that gratification at work and independence on the job were about as important as money in their choice of jobs.[3] A 1989 Gallup Poll found that people who identify with their jobs are happier than those who don't.[4] What made them identify with their work? Strong relationships with other employees at all levels, involvement and input in decision making, and a sense of belonging. Another indicator of job satisfaction — income — was of less importance.

A 1988 *Rolling Stone* magazine survey of job dissatisfaction found that only seven percent of the respondents mentioned low pay or insufficient benefits. But 61 percent felt they weren't treated like professionals. They wanted more respect.[5]

"Today's workers want more freedom, more choice, and more responsibility," says management consultant Donald Clifton. "And it's only in the last few years that managers have come to recognize employee empowerment as an important objective."[6]

RECOGNITION FILLS THE GAP

Today's smart managers recognize that a good job is more than a steady paycheck to America's workers, and that given the opportunity and incentive to participate, employees will respond with enthusiasm. But employee enthusiasm must be nurtured. Recognition reinforces performance and encourages workers to continue to do their best.

"Recognition is something a manager should be doing all the time. It's a running dialogue with people," says Ron Zemke, co-author of *Service America!* and *Managing Knock Your Socks Off Service*, and owner of Performance Research Associates, Minneapolis.[7]

Harvey Stein, owner of a Denver-based incentives company, agrees. "We all like to be recognized and appreciated. Just by giving an award or recognition certificate, formally recognizing someone in front of a group or just buying someone a cup of coffee, we're telling the employees that their work is appreciated even though it might not be measurable."[8]

According to Thomas Kelley, chairman of the board of the Society for Human Resource Management, "What makes employees come to work is a sense of pride, recognition, and achievement. Workers committed to their jobs and recognized for their work will work whatever hours it takes to get the job done."[9]

Reward for a job well done is often cited by experts as a way to increase employee satisfaction even when traditional sources of recognition, like raises or promotions, don't come through. Recognition gives people an opportunity to feel valued by both managers and peers, and it enhances interaction, communication, and team spirit.

JOB STRESS — PRODUCERS AND REDUCERS

To understand how recognition makes a difference we need to examine the pressures on today's workers. Most companies today face economic recession, budget cuts, and the threat of layoffs. Many employees work under a rigid management hierarchy that limits their involvement and participation. The results are lack of motivation, lowered productivity, absenteeism, complaints, and high turnover. These are the elements of job burnout.

The issue of job burnout has become a hot topic in the pages of *Forbes, Fortune,* and other business journals. Stress in the workplace not only cripples workers, it also burdens employers, who are faced with ever-increasing levels of stress-related workers' compensation claims. Stress-related disability cases rose from six percent in 1982 to 13 percent by 1990 (see chart at right), according

Stress-Related Disability Cases

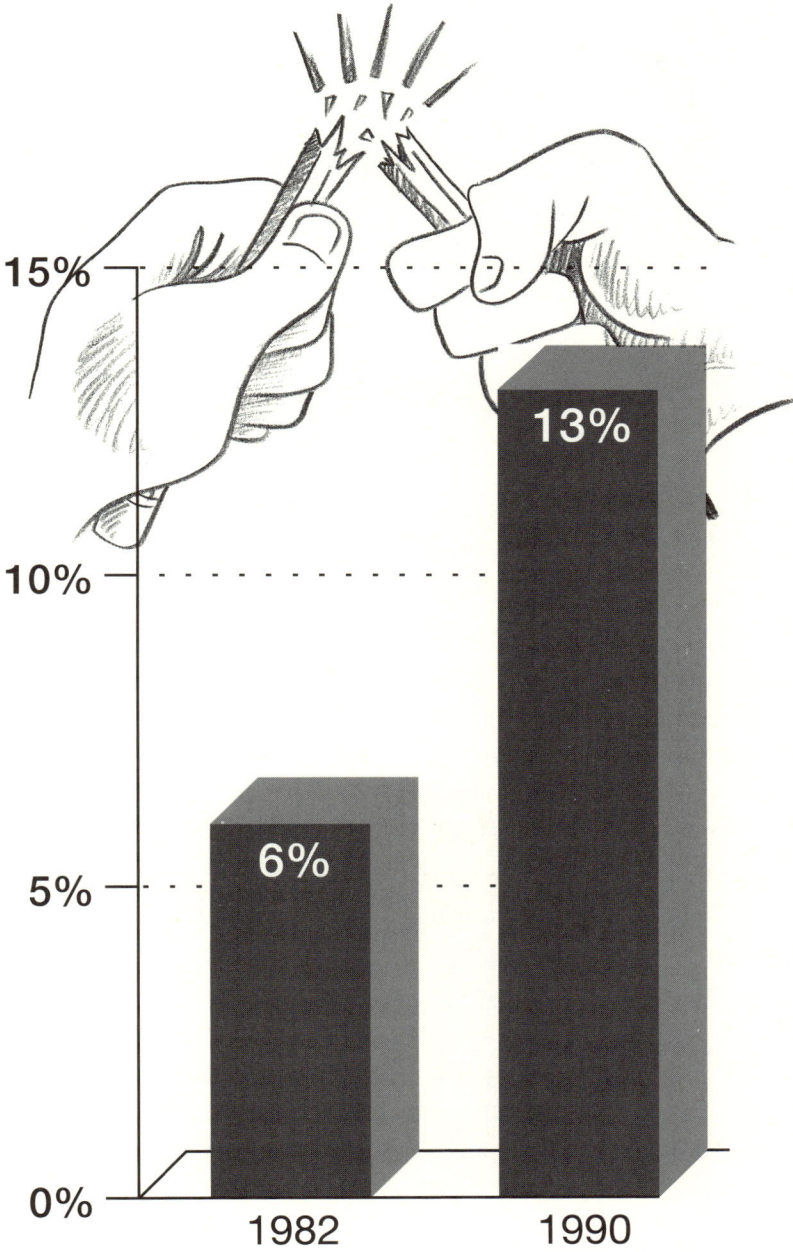

15% ┈┈┈┈┈┈┈┈┈┈┈┈┈┈┈┈┈┈┈┈

13%

10% ┈┈┈┈┈┈┈┈┈┈┈┈┈┈┈┈┈┈┈┈

6%

5% ┈┈┈┈┈┈┈┈┈┈┈┈┈┈┈┈┈┈┈┈

0%

1982   1990

> *"Formal research and informal experience both demonstrate that people who feel appreciated hustle more, treat customers better, and in general provide a higher level of service."*
>
> Marc Hequet
> *Training* Magazine

to a 1991 national survey. In a report entitled "Employee Burnout: America's Newest Epidemic," conducted by Northwestern National Life Insurance of Minneapolis,[10] seven out of 10 workers said job stress lowers their productivity and contributes to health problems. The study also listed stress producers and stress reducers in the work place. Recognition was listed among the nine top stress reducers. Five of the other top stress reducers were related to improved communication and interaction.

THE GOOD, THE BAD, AND THE AWFUL

"If people chronically complain, tell you how bad life is, and how awful things are, it usually means that they want to make you aware of their efforts," says performance management consultant Janis Allen. "When they bellyache, they are getting, in a backhanded way, the attention they weren't getting. They're getting the recognition they want."[11]

Many psychologists believe that complaining is a symptom of something deeper. The complaint is rooted in the person's feeling of helplessness, not pessimism. Complainers may put down others to boost their own self-worth. Or they may be nit-pickers, who constantly find fault with company policies, systems, departments, or managers. Complainers complain to get attention. Besides being annoying, complaining is contagious. It can set the tone for a whole group and lower everyone's feeling of satisfaction. However, if people get recognition, praise, acceptance, and support, they don't need to complain anymore. As they gain the recognition they need, they stop complaining. Their attitude improves and they stop poisoning the environment for others.

INVOLVEMENT MEANS RECOGNITION

For many employees, empowerment is a form of recognition. Having the tools and the authority to achieve results can be exhilarating. When their efforts are successful, employees know that they personally have made a significant contribution. That feels good. And, when an employee is recognized before his or her managers and peers, it's icing on the cake — it validates his or her worth.

> "We know that a majority of the people at Tennant think recognition is worthwhile because they do it."
>
> **John Davis**

"Employee involvement is certainly a part of recognition," says Tennant Vice President Paul Brunelle. "It's the way some people get recognized; it's a way some people get a feeling of belonging; and for some people, that's exactly the recognition they want — to be part of a group."

"With employees on the inside, you have a stronger team, stronger decisions and results, and more commitment," says Gannett Senior Vice President Madelyn Jennings. "People willingly work hard if they're working in that kind of environment."[12] When employees are empowered and become more enthusiastic, creative, and productive, the companies they work for never look back. "I've yet to hear an employee say she'd like to go back to the old way of doing business," says executive consultant John Zenger.[13]

NEW POWER

Employee empowerment does not erode a manager's role or responsibility, but it does demand a change in style and approach. Ken Blanchard describes the new management style as a shift from positional power to personal power. Personal power is the ability to get people to **want** to perform instead of "making" them perform. As leaders give up the use of positional power, they will gain influence by listening and communicating, and by enhancing employee self-esteem.

Through Tennant's quality and recognition processes, we have developed and refined our principles of empowerment, open communication, respect, and recognition. Each is an integrated part of the whole that has led to increased satisfaction among Tennant's workers. The opportunity to make work more satisfying and contribute in a meaningful way to the success of the company is probably the strongest and best reason for a sustained interest in quality at Tennant. "It's hard for me to imagine a successful recognition process unless we also work to strengthen our communication processes," says John Davis, Tennant's director of manufacturing engineering and product conformance. "They go hand in hand."

A SUCCESS STORY

The link between recognition and communication was first demonstrated early in the quality process by an unlikely group of employees, the Tennant welding department. Their story is told in full in *Quest for Quality*, but it is worth summarizing here. In the mid-1970s, these 37 men were the company rebels. Many drove big, chunky Harley-Davidson motorcycles that symbolized their style and image; they wore drab Army-surplus fatigues to protect themselves from flying sparks. (Their

29

unofficial uniform set them apart from the other production workers and added to their mystique.) In 1981, a new supervisor was assigned to the welders who worked the night shift. He took a fresh look at the department's work patterns, and he noticed room for improvement. For example, half an hour of every shift was set aside to change the welding wire on the welding machines. Changing this wire actually took little more than 5 minutes; the welders spent the remaining 25 minutes waiting to resume work. The supervisor suggested they change the wires whenever they needed to instead of waiting for the "official" time, and resume work immediately instead of waiting for 25 minutes. The result was an immediate leap in efficiency for the entire department.

> *"Recognition is a journey of continual improvement. Listening to what people want, what people think, is important. So too is changing and improving the programs to make them more meaningful to people."*
>
> **Paul Brunelle**
> **Tennant**

The supervisor posted a chart that graphically showed the department's improved productivity. Soon, members of the night welding shift began to volunteer other suggestions for improving efficiency. Their ideas led to increased profits for the company, and they used their cash rewards for group camping and boating trips. Slowly, these rugged nonconformists began to work as a team.

During the next year, some members of the night shift crew and their supervisor transferred to the day shift. There the supervisor became interested in a productivity effort called RISLIP (Reduce Inventory, Space, Labor, Improve Productivity) and began to talk with his section workers about how it might be achieved. Originally, the welding process was to work on individual parts of a sweeping or scrubbing machine frame, frame sides, or housings for brushes, for example — then send them to the stockroom until an order was received for a particular machine. The company's engineers wanted to streamline the assembly operation so that fewer units would go into storage. The welders devised a system with a $100,000 price tag that was rejected by management as too expensive. Even a scaled-down $25,000 version was too costly.

A small group of welders tackled the problem. They envisioned an overhead monorail that would carry welded parts from one station to another so that a frame could be welded together from start to finish without leaving the department. The welders then discovered a supply of I-beams in a local junkyard and bought them for less then $2,000. In two days, they installed the monorail. In the first year of use, the new system saved Tennant more than $29,000 in time and storage space.

All this time, the welding supervisor was carefully documenting the cost of quality in his department. In 1981, he calculated, the welding department's annual cost of quality was $73,186. Reworking parts not made right the first time was responsible for most of that cost. A whopping 2,939 hours in 1981 were spent on rework. Within two years, the welders had reduced their cost of quality to $11,794 and rework hours to 249.

These dramatic reductions were achieved by small groups that tackled specific problems — inefficient setups, for instance. In 1982, the welders were setting up their jobs at 54.7 percent of industrial engineering standards for efficiency. A group of five welders, one from each section, met to work out a system for improving that percentage. They made scheduling changes, grouping several small jobs together so they could be done by the same welder. They assigned larger jobs to a single welder who would improve his techniques to save time. One year later, the welders' average setup rate was 78 percent of the engineering standard. The welders kept going. By mid-1984, the welders' setup efficiency had increased to 90 percent, saving $45,000 a year for Tennant. At the same time, a productivity improvement team began converting welding's inventory ordering for major components to a Just-in Time system that saved Tennant $100,000 a year.

What was in it for the welders? Satisfaction. In the words of one team member: "I feel like I'm part owner of this company. I know that if I have a complaint about anything, it will be heard — not always answered to my satisfaction, but heard. I'm going to do anything I can to make this company and the quality process a success. I'm happy being a welder, but when I have an opportunity to be part of a group working in another area, I jump at the chance. I really want to share what I've learned."

INTEGRATING RECOGNITION

The welders' success is one example of how the recognition process at Tennant has inspired creativity and productivity, and instilled a sense of pride and satisfaction among the company's employees.

When recognition has been done thoroughly and systematically, it has helped Tennant achieve outstanding results. Every story is different, of course. Some come from the manufacturing area, others from less quantifiable areas like customer service. But regardless of department or position, employees agree that recognition inspires them to do their best work.

Setting up a program is not enough, however. In a survey by the American Productivity and Quality Center in Houston, 91 percent of the respondents said recognition was a powerful motivator.[14] Even though many work in companies that have established recognition programs, nearly half said they did not receive such recognition. Diversity, flexibility, and thoroughness are necessary to make recognition one of a company's core values. And all forms of recognition — formal, informal, and day-to-day — must be integrated to give employees an understanding of how and why their work is valued.

THE IMPORTANCE OF BASELINE MEASUREMENT

Before a company can implement an effective recognition program, it must incorporate a set of goals and a system of measurement to define the current situation and to guide change. This begins with a baseline measurement, a starting point that provides a framework for measuring improvement, goal achievement, and recognition based on results. "Without goal setting and measurement," says Paul Brunelle, "a recognition program is fairly empty. You're recognizing people for performance, but you don't know if that performance is good or if you're headed in the right direction."

Some goals are based on data — the number of products produced or time saved, the number of claims processed or potential clients called. But others are not so easily quantified. Some issues, such as the quality of customer care, are difficult to measure. At Tennant, we're always striving to improve our ability to measure change. "Once you set goals, then you've got to measure your performance against them. When you meet your goals, then you recognize that achievement," says Brunelle. "They tie together."

LOOKING INSIDE THE MIND

A true understanding of the importance of recognition requires that we examine the complex issues of human motivation and behavior. What guides our thinking processes, our feelings, and our actions? Social scientists, psychologists, and behaviorists have grappled with these questions for years. As a result, a number of theories have emerged that attempt to explain and predict human behavior under a variety of circumstances. We will examine them in the next chapter.

What Happens When There is No Recognition

Company A doesn't have a recognition program. Recognition is absent from the corporate culture and management is skeptical of the whole concept. Work is work, says the CEO, who achieved success through the "school of hard knocks." The company is in business to do business, he believes. The employees receive a steady job and decent pay in exchange for their commitment. What more do they want?

Plenty, according to communications consultant Dr. Alan R. Zimmerman,[15] and an examination of Company A proves it. Without proper recognition, many employees will simply quit and look for another job. Or they'll call in sick frequently. They interview for a new job on company time and when they find one, they quit. The company faces the long and expensive process of advertising vacancies, paying employment agency fees, and training a new employee. Add to these obvious costs the time managers spend reviewing resumes and interviewing candidates, plus lost productivity while the position goes unfilled and the new worker gets up to speed.

Chances are, the new person won't last long, and the company is back to square one.

More than likely, the person who quit was a good employee — most people who leave their jobs are. In 1988, *Personnel Journal* reported that 92 percent of 900 salaried/exempt employees who resigned were ranked as "satisfactory" or better performers.[16] Clearly, companies with high turnover are losing valuable talent. A 1989 survey by Motivational Systems, a corporate management development and sales organization, revealed that 25 million Americans find not being appreciated at work a valid reason for finding a new job. The survey also showed that 38 percent of all employees said that they seldom or never receive recognition from their bosses.[17]

But what if the employee needs the job and can't go elsewhere? He or she stays and keeps drawing paychecks. Does that mean everything is okay? Not necessarily.

The worker may become apathetic and disinterested in the job and the well-being of the company. After all, "If the company doesn't care about me," the worker may reason, "why should I care about it?" Such an attitude will inspire only minimal effort from most employees — just enough to get by. When on the job, work standards are lax.

Some dissatisfied workers take a more aggressive approach by rebelling against the company. Workers who feel they have been treated unfairly may sabotage the company to "balance the scales." Some may become chronic blamers or complainers. Others may pilfer office supplies or steal more expensive company property. Still others may attempt to bring about change. One might bring in the union for a confrontation or try to alter the rules. Others may try to sanction what they want to do informally, possibly by lowering standards of production.

In addition to these dysfunctional behaviors, most workers will develop feelings of conflict and frustration. When the basic psychological need for recognition is not met, self-esteem is undermined. Employees lose their sense of self-worth, and doubt that their contributions have value. They stop trying. After all, people won't continue to give when they get little in return.

❖

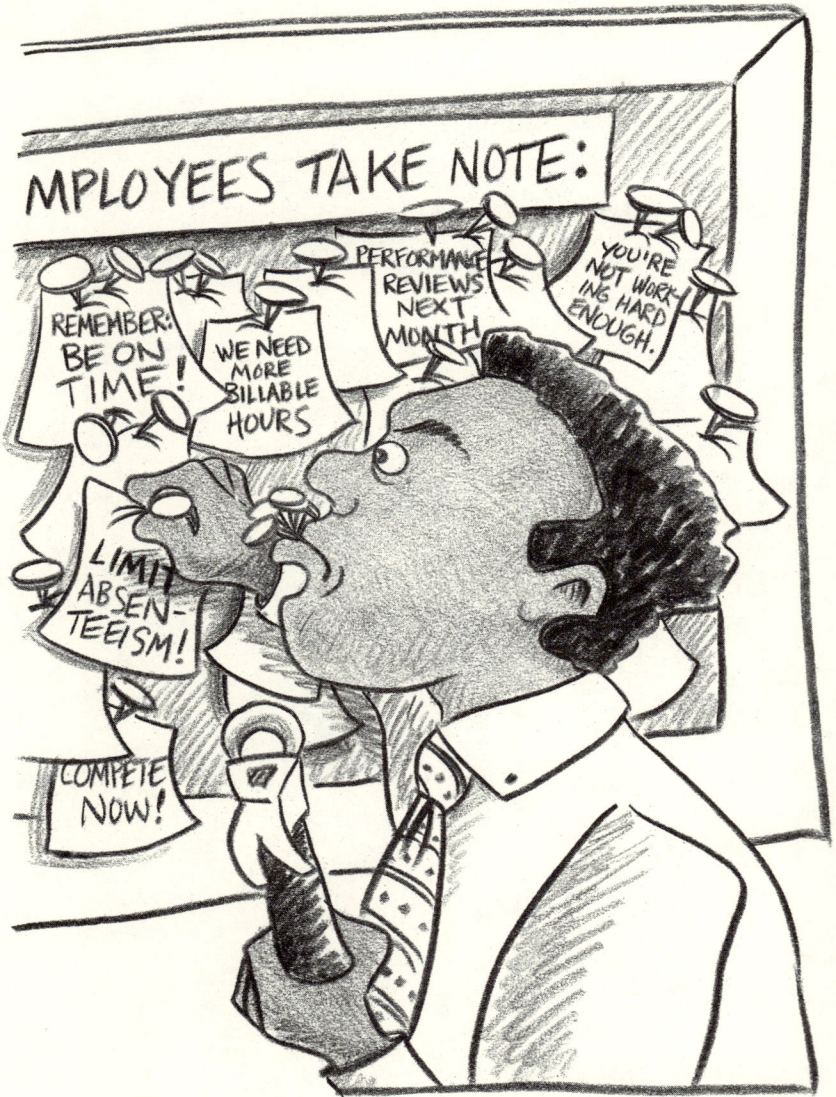

When the only tool one has is a hammer, one tends to treat all problems as nails.

Chapter 3

Behaviorists' Theories on Recognition

Surveys and studies of employee attitudes and our own experiences at Tennant strongly suggest that recognition is valued by employees. It is so valued that it enhances employee self-esteem and personal satisfaction. Recognition improves productivity on the job and helps limit absenteeism, job turnover, and other organizational problems. Recognition is important. But what niche should it fill? And how is it linked with behavior?

SCIENCE STEPS IN

In school we learned that the scientific method is a system of goals and measurements tied to consistency. We conducted experiments and controlled variables so we could replicate results. That's the way we learned how the world works.

Like biology, chemistry, or physics, the scientific study of the human mind is enormously complex. Each of us is a unique combination of traits and characteristics, and multitudinous variables. We often don't understand ourselves, much less society at large. Is it possible to subject human behavior to precise and consistent scientific measurement?

A number of pioneering behavioral scientists have attempted to do just that — often with great success. Some have taken the broad theoretical approach, proposing theories that attempt to rationally explain the multilayered system of human needs and desires. Others have taken a narrow approach, predicting behavior through rigorous experimentation. As a result, a number of behavioral scientists with varying styles and ideas have led the scientific study of motivation and behavior.

MASLOW'S HIERARCHY

> *"When the only tool one has is a hammer, one tends to treat all problems as nails."*
>
> **Abraham Maslow**

Anyone who took Psychology 101 in college should recall the work of A. H. Maslow. Building on the classical studies of psychology, experimental psychology, and psychoanalysis developed by Freud, Adler, and Jung, Maslow took a holistic approach to human needs in his famous theory, "The Hierarchy of Basic Human Needs."

Physiological needs: air, water, and food.

Safety needs: adequate shelter, clothing, and job security.

Social needs: love and affection, belonging, and acceptance by others.

Ego needs: a positive self-image and self-respect, recognition from others — achievement, status, and appreciation.

Self-Actualization needs: the ability to fully realize one's potential, through continued growth and individual development.

According to Maslow's theory, people's needs begin at the most fundamental level. They must satisfy these basic needs before moving up to the next stage. The need for food and shelter must be met before people can concern themselves with fulfilling their needs at succeeding levels (see pyramid at right).

Maslow's Hierarchy

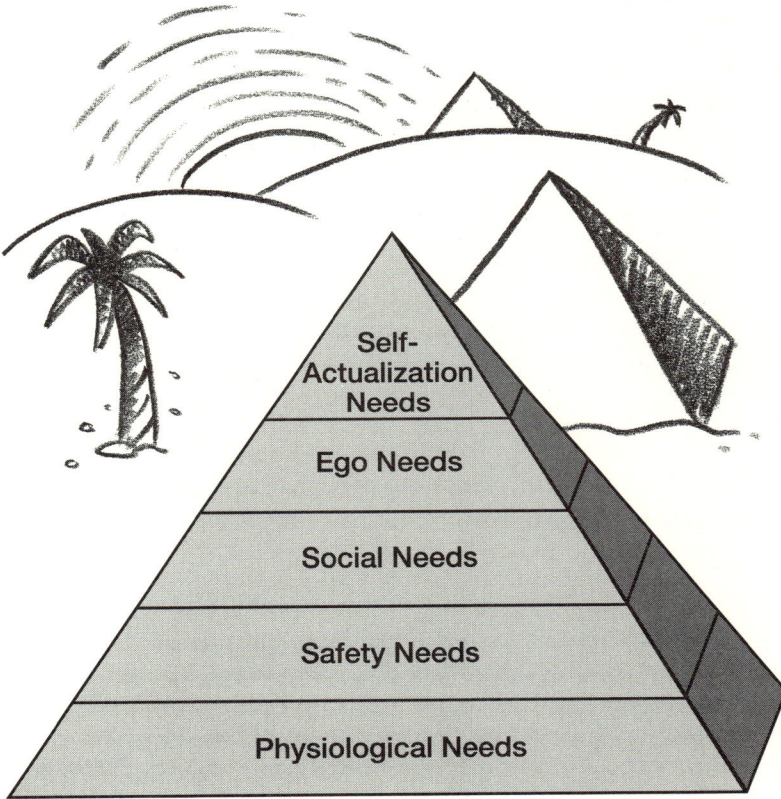

Maslow describes the first three levels of his hierarchy as basic or deficit needs. The third level includes the need for acceptance and belonging, crucial facets of self-esteem and satisfaction. Recognition is identified at the fourth level, among the ego needs. The sense of achievement and appreciation that derives from recognition leads to the pinnacle of Maslow's hierarchy — self-actualization.

Other researchers have adapted this hierarchy specifically to the organizational setting. Redefining the hierarchy in these terms reveals how a person's work contributes to satisfying his or her needs:

Physiological needs: An organization provides a clean, comfortable environment with adequate facilities.

Safety needs: An employer provides safe equipment and machinery, safety procedures and precautions; job continuity gives workers a feeling of security from layoffs, and grievance systems protect them from arbitrary actions.

Social needs: An organization provides opportunities for employees to work together on teams or work groups in which they interact with one another.

Ego needs: An employer provides workers with challenges and responsibilities, which are opportunities for achievement. Recognition of achievement reinforces the employee's feeling of accomplishment and makes him or her feel appreciated.

Self-actualization needs: Some researchers believe that this need cannot be achieved from the workplace, but must come from within the individual. Others believe employers can contribute to employee self-actualization by providing employees with opportunities for learning, decision-making, and promotion.[1]

HERZBERG'S TWO-FACTOR THEORY

To understand the work of Frederick Herzberg, we must put aside Maslow's ascending needs theory and grasp the concept of a two-dimensional needs system. We can visualize job satisfaction in two dimensions if it is portrayed as a spectrum, with satisfaction and dissatisfaction at opposite ends. Most employees would fall somewhere along the line between highly satisfied and totally dissatisfied.

According to researcher Herzberg, to increase job satisfaction, an employer would have to first overcome the dissatisfiers and then provide motivators.

One dimension consists of factors related to the work environment, not the work itself. These extrinsic factors, which include salary, working conditions, and supervision, do not contribute to job satisfaction, even when they are met. On the contrary, when these factors are met, they merely enable the employee to avoid unpleasantness.

If work factors are not met, if the pay is poor, the working conditions bad, or the supervision harsh, the employee will be dissatisfied and forced into an unpleasant situation. No amount of motivation will overcome the problem.

On the other hand, when an employee has an adequate salary, good working conditions, and good supervision — the factors will be met and his rating on the scale will be the best it can be — no dissatisfaction. But that's not the same as satisfaction, is it?

That's where Herzberg's motivation factors come in. These factors pertain directly to satisfaction, and they are related specifically to work content. Motivation factors are intrinsic to the work itself, to achievement, and to recognition. When met, they fulfill an individual's need for psychological growth. Herzberg represents this with a continuum ranging from satisfaction to "no" satisfaction.

APPLYING HERZBERG

According to Herzberg, motivating employees is a two-step process. First, the manager ensures that the hygiene factors, the potential dissatisfiers, are met. This does not stimulate motivation, but ensures that employees do not become dissatisfied. It is the starting point. Next, the manager gives the employee the motivators — such as recognition. This ultimately leads to increased job satisfaction.

In *Work and the Nature of Man,* Herzberg explained his complex theory with a simple analogy: "Let us characterize job satisfaction as vision and job dissatisfaction as hearing. [These] are...two separate dimensions, since the stimulus for vision is light, and increasing and decreasing light will have no effect on one's hearing. The stimulus for hearing is sound, and in a similar fashion, increasing or decreasing loudness will have no effect on vision." Using Herzberg's analogy, if you want employees to be satisfied, raising their pay may not be what they need. That's just turning on the lights to make them hear better. That's what many companies have been doing for years.

APPLICATION OF MASLOW AND HERZBERG

"Organizations in the U.S. industrial sector have done a better job of satisfying the extrinsic or hygienic needs of their workers than they have in satisfying the intrinsic or self-fulfillment needs," wrote management researcher Kenneth A. Kovach,[2] after reviewing 40 years of research on what employees want.

Both Maslow and Herzberg would certainly agree. Maslow would point out that employers aim too low, concerning themselves with lower level needs of survival and safety (a clean, safe work area and steady pay). Employers should aim at the upper need levels. Herzberg would say that many employers aim at the extrinsic needs and overlook the motivators — the only route to job satisfaction.

While both Maslow and Herzberg offer useful insights into factors that inspire motivation, neither theorist tackled the process of motivation. Do different workers want different things? Why? How does an organization motivate its employees? How is motivation sustained? How can the results be measured? And how can the results be repeated?

Researchers have known the answers to some of these questions for years, but spreading the word has been a bit more difficult.

WHAT DO EMPLOYEES REALLY WANT?

In 1946, in the midst of new discoveries on motivation by behavioral scientists, a major U.S. corporation conducted a survey of industrial employees, asking them to rank 10 "job reward" factors. The question researchers were attempting to answer was "What do employees want? What factors provide the most job satisfaction?" Here were the 1946 rankings:

1. Full appreciation of work done
2. Feeling of being in on things
3. Sympathetic help with personal problems
4. Job security
5. Good wages
6. Interesting work
7. Promotion/growth in the organization
8. Personal loyalty to employees
9. Good working conditions
10. Tactful discipline

The same survey, given to industrial employees in 1981, produced similar results. After nearly 40 years, there were only a few changes. "Interesting work," which had been in the number five in 1946, rose to the number one position in 1981, while number 3, "sympathetic help with personal problems," dropped to ninth position.

In 1986, industrial workers participating in the survey ranked their preferences in roughly the same order as the 1981 group:

1. Interesting work
2. Full appreciation of work done
3. Feeling of being in on things
4. Job security
5. Good wages
6. Promotion/growth in the organization
7. Good working conditions
8. Personal loyalty to employees
9. Tactful discipline
10. Sympathetic help with personal problems

A comparison of employees in the 1940s and the 1980s shows that they have been remarkably consistent in describing what they felt was important. Scientists attributed the two major changes, a decline in the importance of "sympathetic help with personal problems" and a rise in the importance of "interesting work," as natural products of the times. Many employees in 1946 had suffered through the Depression and World War II. By the 1980s, four decades of prosperity and a dramatic rise in the American standard of living had significantly altered the daily life of the typical American worker. But the workers' need for recognition remains constant.[3]

SUPERVISORS' PERCEPTIONS

What good does it do if researchers know what the employee wants? One important benefit is that an employee's company and, more important, an employee's supervisor are in the position to meet the employee's needs. But does the supervisor automatically know what the employee wants? Are they on the same wavelength?

To explore these questions, researchers gave the same survey to supervisors — with a twist. Instead of ranking their own preferences, the supervisors ranked the job rewards the way they thought their employees would rank them. Like the employees, the supervisors' rankings in 1946, 1981, and 1986 were consistent — in fact nearly identical for all three rankings. But in each survey, as you can see, the supervisors' perceptions were dramatically different from their workers' preferences.

1. Good wages
2. Job security
3. Promotion and growth in the organization
4. Good working conditions
5. Interesting work
6. Personal loyalty to employees
7. Tactful discipline
8. Full appreciation of work done
9. Sympathetic help with personal problems
10. Feeling of being in on things

Unfortunately, while supervisors had a consistent perception of employees' needs over the 40-year period, those perceptions were just as consistently off the mark. The fact that supervisors rated their employees' top three motivating factors as numbers 5, 8, and 10, respectively, indicate that supervisors have an inaccurate perception of what motivates employees. And nearly 40 years of research has done little to change those perceptions.[4]

Numerous similar employee surveys conducted by companies throughout the country have come up with the same questions and received the same answers. Workers responding to a 1989 survey listed honest company communications and respectful treatment of employees among the top five attributes of a good employer. Good pay ranked 11th.[5]

Somehow the wealth of information generated by all this research has been ignored by many organizations. With such limited understanding between groups of people who work closely together, major problems, like the recent decline in American productivity, should come as no great surprise. According to figures quoted in the April 17, 1989, issue of *Business Week,* U.S. production rose only about 1 percent per year between 1973 and 1989 — compared to 2.7 percent annually for the previous 15 years.

> *"People don't change their behavior unless it makes a difference for them to do so."*
>
> **Fran Tarkenton**
> **Tarkenton & Co.,**
> **Atlanta**

But wait! We've known what employees have wanted for 40 years. Why has employee productivity dropped only recently? Many researchers believe this phenomenon can be explained by a change in employee expectations.

A 1980s follow-up to a mid-1950s study revealed that employees' expectations have dramatically altered during that 25-year period. The attitude survey, which was given among several companies, found that although clerical and hourly employees considered their salaries adequate, they were becoming increasingly dissatisfied with the company's ability to be fair, respectful, and responsive.

The same study showed that the number of managers and clerical employees who rated their companies as 'very good' or 'good' in these categories in 1950-59 plummeted to half the '50s' total in 1975-77. Researchers see this as a change in workers' values: "All parts of the work force are beginning to overtly articulate their needs for achievement, recognition, and job challenge," said M. R. Cooper and the other authors of the 1979 report.[6]

REVIEWING MASLOW & WHAT WORKERS WANT

Decades of attitude research support what Maslow and Herzberg proposed years ago. It seems clear that educating supervisors on the values and needs of employees and finding practical ways to implement the theories of the two scientists are the essentials of success. Recognition is cited by theorists as a primary means of fostering an atmosphere of trust and respect among employees. It gives them a feeling of independence and control, and enhances their self-esteem. It helps create an environment where there is little to lose and much to gain.

But recognition must be linked to performance if it is to be meaningful for the individual. And it must reinforce desired behaviors in order to have value for the organization. A new generation of scientists, psychologists, and researchers has scientifically linked recognition to behavior and performance. Let's take a look at how they did it.

SKINNER AND BEHAVIOR

Psychologist B. F. Skinner was instrumental in bringing the study of behavior from the theoretical to the scientific level. He used research techniques to precisely measure animal behavior that can be applied successfully to human behavior.

One technique is called "response shaping." Skinner placed a rat in a box fitted with a lever mounted high on the wall. He assumed that the rat was unlikely to press the lever when it was first put in the box. Each time the rat moved closer to the intended goal, it was rewarded with food. Skinner didn't wait for perfect behavior to reward the animal. He rewarded progress. In a very short time, Skinner's rats were pushing the lever. He had shaped their behavior.

Skinner also made important contributions to our understanding of motivation and productivity. Using what he called "schedules of reinforcement," he trained animals to change their behavior and improve their productivity.

In a series of experiments, Skinner and his colleagues set up several different types of reinforcement schedules. In one instance, a food pellet was given to a pigeon every time it pecked a window. This was called a continuous schedule of reinforcement. Another pigeon received reinforcement at variably timed intervals. This was a variable ratio schedule. Each schedule created predictable patterns of behavior. They also created unique behavioral consequences.

Skinner first noted these consequences in the pigeons set on the variable ratio (VR) schedule. One morning, Skinner found his pigeons behaving strangely. One was bobbing up and down, another was twisting its head, and the third was rubbing itself against the floor. At first, Skinner didn't understand what was going on. Then he noticed that a fault in his electrical circuits was causing his experimental boxes to occasionally deliver food pellets whether or not the pigeons pecked the window. So, if one pigeon just happened to bob its head when the pellet was delivered, it continued to bob its head until another pellet was accidentally delivered. Skinner called this reaction superstitious behavior.

Scientists have found that both animals and people like to work on the VR schedule more than any other, possibly because of the excitement induced by the promise of a payoff at any minute. When combined with accidental occurrences, a VR schedule promotes superstitious behavior. A stroll through a gambling casino will confirm the application of his conclusions to human behavior.

Skinner also found characteristic patterns of behavior in the other schedules of reinforcement. Pigeons working on high fixed ratios (FR) would quit working for a long time after getting several food pellets. If the ratio was too high, the pigeon lost its motivation altogether and Skinner had a hard time getting it back to work.

Researchers say that the behavior Skinner observed in these pigeons has a correlation with piece-work factory employees in the early 1900s. They also worked on a fixed-rate system. The factory workers' low level of productivity eventually forced their employers to abandon piece-work schedules. Investigating the behavior years later, Skinner learned how to overcome the negative effects of these FR schedules. With food pellet rewards, he provided his pigeons with frequent, cumulative feedback about their progress throughout the work schedule.

HAWTHORNE AND PRODUCTIVITY

Much of Skinner's work with schedules is directly applicable to the work situation. For example, organizations are beginning to learn that the poor information and incentives found in many traditional company hierarchies contribute significantly to low productivity.

Skinner's work in motivation and productivity helped industrial psychologist H. M. Parsons solve the mystery of the "Hawthorne Effect." Years ago, psychologists in a Western Electric plant conducted an experiment on worker productivity. They introduced into the work environment a variety of distracting conditions to see what effects they had on the work rate. For the "experimental workers," the heat was turned up or turned down; levels of noise and light were altered daily. Regardless of the changes, however, productivity was consistently 50 percent higher for these experimental workers. At the time, scientists believed that paying attention to the employees increased their productivity.

Years later, Parsons re-analyzed the original data and found two things the original researchers had overlooked. First, the supervisor in the experimental room had mounted a counter in front of each assembler to monitor her productivity. For the first time, the employee could note her progress. Second, the supervisor had arranged to pay the assemblers on the basis of their production rather than on a fixed schedule.

As a result of those changes, productivity increased. During the 20 years of data collection, only when the counter malfunctioned did productivity in the experimental room fall to the factory average. Continuous positive reinforcement, as Skinner had observed, accounted for the change.[7]

WORKING BACKWARDS

How did Skinner's methods differ from those of other scientists? Skinner worked backwards. He didn't introduce his subjects to random variables and observe changes in their behavior. Instead, he determined what particular behavior he wanted his subjects to achieve — pulling a lever or pecking a window. Then he investigated ways to best produce that behavior. Skinner's approach has been lauded and adapted by psychologists, consultants, and management experts, many of whom are leaders in the field today.

KEN BLANCHARD AND GOALS

Author Ken Blanchard once wrote: "Imagine yourself as a top athlete trying out for the Olympics, but not knowing how high you jumped or how fast you ran. It seems laughable. Yet many managers fail to tell their people anything about their on-the-job performance."

In a nutshell, that's the problem. Blanchard's solution includes recognition as one of its three key elements. In his best-selling book, *The One Minute Manager*, Blanchard spells out the three simple techniques that work — one-minute goals, one-minute praising, and one-minute reprimands.

Goal setting, Blanchard says, clearly spells out employees' job responsibilities and what they are being held accountable for. This "no surprises" approach lets everyone know what behaviors are expected at the beginning.

In addition to setting down the goals, the manager defines standards for good performance. Expectations are laid out. They are short and simple. They are referenced to help employees keep track of their performance.

Second, one-minute praising gives employees clear feedback on their performance — immediately, specifically, and consistently. This lets employees know how they're performing and helps them feel good when they're doing things right and making progress toward the goal. Like Skinner, Blanchard found that rewarding progress — instead of waiting for perfect performance — helps shape desired behaviors.

> *"Help people reach their full potential: Catch them doing something right."*
>
> **Ken Blanchard,**
> **co-author,**
> **The One Minute Manager**

Even Blanchard's one-minute reprimand offers an opportunity for support. Like praise, the reprimand is immediate, specific, and directed at a behavior, not the person. It's followed by praise — letting the employee know he or she is valued.

PERFORMANCE MANAGEMENT

Recognition is also central to Performance Management, a concept developed by psychologist Aubrey C. Daniels about 20 years ago. Like the ideas originated by Skinner and Blanchard, Performance Management is based on positive reinforcement as a key to employee motivation.

According to Daniels, there are two types of performance problems in organizations: the "can't do" and the "won't do." Can't-do problems are related to knowledge or skill. They can be addressed through employee training. Won't-do problems are rooted in motivation, and are the cause of poor performance.

In his book, *Performance Management,*[8] Daniels quotes a 1983 study by Yankelovich and Immerwhar on American competitive vitality. Only 23 percent of the employees surveyed said they were performing at full capacity and being fully effective. Nearly half the respondents — 44 percent — said they put less effort into their jobs than was required. The majority said they could increase their effectiveness significantly. Obviously these people were aware of their behavior. Most of them were not motivated to give more because something was missing.

"A person's need for positive reinforcement is similar to business's need for profit," says Daniels. Wages and financial benefits are necessary for economic survival, but money alone doesn't inspire a person to maintain peak performance. Only positive reinforcement can do that.

HOW DOES IT WORK?

The practice of performance management uses Skinner's discoveries about human behavior and motivation to systematically oversee employees' work performance. Managers determine the results they are seeking, identify the behaviors necessary to accomplish those results, then measure the performance to determine when to give the employee the positive reinforcement he or she needs to improve and maximize that performance.

Like Skinner, performance management researchers have found that positive feedback is the most effective way to help people achieve work-related goals. It helps shape desired behavior and then strengthens or maximizes existing performance. It also creates a win/win situation. The employee receives reinforcement or recognition for his or her accomplishments and the organization enjoys the benefits of top employee performance.

REINFORCEMENT OR RECOGNITION

Though we've used the terms positive reinforcement and recognition almost interchangeably, there is a difference between the two, and it is specifically related to time. Researchers define positive reinforcement as the feedback a person receives during or immediately after his or her behavior. Recognition occurs sometime later.

Though it is preferable to reinforce a behavior as soon as it occurs, it is not always possible to do so at work. Besides, some work is long-term. Some of it is a result of team effort. That's why different types of recognition — formal, informal, and day-to-day — are so important. They cover the full spectrum of circumstances at work.

But before we examine them in detail, let's first look at the various attributes of recognition.

What Do Employees Want— Young vs. Old

When supervisors in the 1940s and 1980s said money was the most important thing workers wanted, they were right on target with the following groups of employees:

- those under age 30;
- those earning less than $12,000 a year; and
- those at the lower organizational levels.

These findings support Maslow's claim that basic needs must be met before one becomes concerned with the higher needs. A look at these three employee groups shows that they are still trying to cope with basic needs — maybe not for survival, but at least for security. On the average, young employees tend to be lower on the organizational ladder, they earn less, and they haven't yet experienced any real job security. The interesting work, appreciation, and feeling of being in on things lay one or two steps ahead for this group.

Other studies have found differences among employees in different age groups, and the consensus seems to be that people's needs change from one age to another. But a closer look reveals that age isn't the primary factor — the stage of a person's career is what makes the difference.

Most people in the **early stages of their careers** tend to be younger and more concerned with:

- promotion and advancement;
- friendship;
- money; and
- developing their skills.

Recognition is mentioned as a factor, but not as the primary focus of work.

On the other hand, **more well-established workers,** between the age of 40 and 55, value:

- achievement;
- independence;
- power and prestige; and
- self-actualization.

Financial considerations in this group cease to be the focus of their careers. (Besides, they tend to make more anyway.)

That doesn't mean recognition is not important to all groups — regardless of age or status. It is. Recognition enhances employee satisfaction and performance at every level. But it is important to provide a wide range of recognition. As the saying goes: different strokes for different folks.[9]

❖

We've learned that recognition cannot be doled out — one-size-fits-all — for every person or situation.

Chapter 4

Attributes of Recognition

Up until now, we've discussed the tremendous impact recognition has on employee attitudes and behavior. Recognition builds and strengthens employee self-esteem. And healthy self-esteem ultimately translates into increased employee satisfaction, motivation, and productivity. When these positive traits are nurtured through recognition, problems like employee complaints, grievances, absenteeism, and turnover decline significantly.

In Chapter 3, we examined the theoretical foundation of recognition. Psychological theorists specifically list recognition among the basic human needs that lead to individual growth and development. Behaviorists and experimental psychologists cite recognition as a powerful motivating force in shaping behavior. Whatever their approach, scientists unraveling the secrets of the human mind have found that recognition, handled correctly, creates a substantial improvement in work performance.

But handling recognition correctly is difficult. In our experience at Tennant, we've learned that recognition cannot be doled out — one-size-fits-all — for every person or situation. People are different from each other, and require different types of recognition.

Numerous variables complicate the recognition process. Some are related to an employee's personality or career status.

Others are tied to particular work situations. Individuals, teams, or groups need different types of recognition. Small daily successes require an approach that differs from the recognition given to someone meeting a major long-term goal. The variations are endless.

Since 1989, when we began working with other organizations on their recognition plans, many have asked us about the distinction between the terms rewards, awards, recognition, and incentives.

The terms used to describe different types of recognition can be confusing. What some authorities refer to as recognition, others define as rewards. There are awards and incentives. Are these all the same things? Sometimes yes, sometimes no. Before we move on to the attributes of recognition, let's define our terms.

RECOGNITION DEFINED

At Tennant, we look at recognition in two ways. On the one hand, we define recognition as a broad, all-encompassing process that boosts employee self-esteem and builds an environment of trust, respect, and independence throughout the company. Recognition in this broad sense can be formal, informal, or day-to-day. It includes the full breadth of recognition opportunities a company has developed to foster a sense of empowerment and ownership in the creative process. It is a means to bind people together through expressed appreciation for a job well done.

On the other hand, we have a more specific definition of recognition at Tennant: Recognition is an action or activity, and as such, it is non-monetary. Non-monetary recognition, we have found, is one of the most powerful motivators in the workplace. It makes people feel good, adds enjoyment to work, and increases their satisfaction.

REWARDS AND INCENTIVES

Unlike pure recognition, rewards or incentives are tangible, and often monetary, ways to recognize a particular performance. They may be cash, merchandise, tickets to a ballgame, or extra time off. "If you do this, then you'll get that" is the rule of incentives. They reward the achievement of a specific goal or milestone — like a sales contest. They can be instituted when a manager is introducing change and new expectations for employees. Incentives help teach people how to accomplish their new goals quickly,

> *Recognition = Action*
> *Reward = Item*

by giving them feedback for particular behaviors or performances. Rewards and incentives may be instituted to heighten employee awareness of new work standards or goals, or to change employee behavior.

A 1987 study, "People, Performance and Pay," conducted by the American Productivity Center in Houston and the American Compensation Association, found that only 19 percent of service companies offered performance incentives, compared to 48 percent of manufacturers.[1] This highlights the difficulties managers face in measuring the performance of administrative and other non-sales employees.

The use of rewards and incentives is more difficult than it seems. Not only must the employee value the reward as a form of recognition, but the reward must be linked to the performance it seeks to reinforce. It must also fit the corporate culture.

Experts say that the wrong recognition may be worse than none at all. This is particularly true of rewards. According to Ron Zemke, rewards must pass the "snicker test."[2] If employees regard the rewards as juvenile or see little value in the merchandise or prize offered, their opinion is likely to show, and the program is bound to fail. The important thing to remember is that a reward is considered a reward only when the recipient perceives it as such.

Toward that end, some companies let employees choose their own rewards. At Tennant, rewards and incentives are the foundation of our informal recognition program. The variety of rewards offered means there is something for everyone to enjoy and appreciate. We'll discuss some of these ideas in Chapter 6.

AWARDS AS RECOGNITION SYMBOLS

At Tennant, we have awards that are associated with our formal recognition programs: The Award of Excellence and the Koala T. Bear Award are our most prestigious symbols of achievement. Those selected to receive these formal awards must go through lengthy and detailed nomination and selection procedures. Though both programs offer gifts to the recipients, the programs are still non-monetary. Being chosen to receive the award is a major achievement. The gifts, which are company-oriented, serve mainly as tangible reminders of the achievement and recognition. We'll discuss our formal recognition awards in detail in Chapter 5.

WHAT ABOUT MONEY?

Is money an effective form of recognition? After all, everyone needs it. If we give money as recognition, would we simplify recognition for everyone involved?

The question of whether money should be used for recognition is a frequent topic among managers and supervisors who want to provide meaningful recognition to their employees. At Tennant, we have also studied the subject's pros and cons and come to the conclusion that money can be effectively used in some instances, but it is not usually the best way to recognize employees. Other companies, including Centel, Rochester Telephone Corp., Kayser-Roth Corporation, and Milliken, agree. The problems are numerous:

1. Cash burns a hole in your pocket. When gone, it's quickly forgotten, leaving no reminder of the recognition it was intended to highlight.

2. Often someone receiving cash will equate the amount with the value of his or her performance. In such a case, the dollar amount will seem minuscule compared to the person's value as an employee. The person will look at the cash and say to himself, "Is that all they think I'm worth?" This not only diminishes the impact of the recognition, but may seem like a punishment.

3. A high cash incentive can cause problems among employees. It often breeds competition that undermines the teamwork necessary to accomplish the company's goals. It causes some employees to lose sight of work goals and focus more on the personal stake they have in winning the money.[3]

Besides these problems, studies have shown that money has less power to motivate people than other types of recognition. The "People, Performance and Pay" study on incentives found that it takes five to eight percent of an employee's salary to change behavior if the reward is given in cash. If a non-cash reward is given, a value approximating four percent of the employee's salary will motivate a change.

> *"It's the employee's perception of the rewards' value that is pivotal in determining worker motivation and satisfaction."*
>
> **Philip C. Grant, Ph.D.**[4]

Other factors related to traditional business practices discourage the potential benefit of monetary recognition. For example, if an employee is given a 10 percent raise in salary in recognition for achievement, will the extra money motivate the person to continue to do his or her best on the job? Not at all, says Ken Blanchard. The problem, he says, is that most organizations' performance reviews, and the corresponding salary increases, occur only once a year. To motivate employees, managers must recognize achievement and progress toward goals much more often. From the manager's point of view, recognition is important because it reinforces desirable behaviors. It lets employees know they are performing well. So it must be done often to motivate employees to consistently achieve.[5] How many managers have pockets full of cash to hand out on a regular basis?

Herzberg, whose theories we examined in the last chapter, studied the relationship between pay and work and found that money was a major factor in job satisfaction when pay was so inadequate that it threatened employee security. Otherwise, pay didn't make an employee happier in the job. When used as a form of recognition, cash only improved feelings of job satisfaction for three to 10 days after a raise. Herzberg found that a sense of achievement and recognition for a job well done were stronger motivators than more money.

THE BEST COMBINATION

Recognition, rewards, awards, incentives — there's a place for each in most organizations. While Tennant likes to emphasize non-monetary recognition, the company backs it up with tangible rewards. We know that a combination of recognition elements is necessary to form a complete program. And it's always important to remember that a recognition program is part of the larger, overall effort toward customer satisfaction — quality in products, service, safety, productivity — that ultimately improves the entire company.

We do have three long-standing recognition programs that award cash to company employees. The safety program, for example, has been in existence for decades. It awards cash bonuses to individuals in departments that avoid lost-time injuries.

Tennant's suggestion program gives cash to employees who submit ideas resulting in cost savings for the company. Both programs were established long before Tennant adopted its three-dimensional recognition model, and they are a small part of our recognition efforts. We'll explain more about the suggestion program in Chapter 5 and the safety program in Chapter 6.

The Tennant Profit Sharing and Employee Stock Ownership Plan (ESOP) are designed so that eligible employees can:

- share in the company's value;
- acquire an ownership interest in the company; and
- have an additional retirement income source.

Profit Sharing contributions, which are stock and cash, are made by the company based on annual return and real sales growth. Since the ESOP also rewards performance, if employees help improve profits, they also may share in larger company contributions to the Plan.

Now that we've gotten our basic definitions straight, let's take a look at the attributes of recognition that help us define and shape the three types of recognition in Tennant's three-dimensional model: formal, informal, and day-to-day recognition.

ATTRIBUTES OF RECOGNITION

It's easy to see how the proliferation of terms and definitions regarding recognition can make the process confusing. To keep us on track in developing and implementing our program, Tennant has devised a list of attributes regarding recognition that helps us differentiate between formal, informal, and day-to-day recognition. To give us a common understanding of these terms, we have also defined each attribute.

Consistent

For recognition to be consistent, it must be delivered the same way every time.

Cost

Recognition items can be inexpensive. Many, like a note, carry almost no price tag at all. However, to serve the needs of everyone in an organization and to ensure that most employees receive some form of recognition, some financial investment is necessary to implement a full-scale recognition program.

Frequent

By frequent recognition, we mean that it occurs often. Some recognition forms — by design — allow more chance of frequency.

Interpersonal Skills

For each kind of recognition, it is essential that the person giving the recognition possess a variety of interpersonal skills. Often the fewer people being recognized, the higher the level of skill necessary to communicate effectively. For example, if a supervisor is recognizing 10 employees at a company meeting, the supervisor will make a brief prepared speech about the total group's accomplishments, and congratulate the group publicly on its efforts. With one-on-one recognition, the supervisor must not only be specific, but "personal" about the individual's accomplishments. The more personalized recognition adds another dimension to the communication. Some people find it difficult to face someone and say, "I like what you did, and here's why."

From Peers

When recognition comes from peers, someone in the employee's peer group takes the initiative to share with others the work done by a co-worker or a group. Extending beyond co-workers at the peer level, we could also include input from direct reports or customers to round out this attribute. This may be shared through formal nominations or more spontaneously through positive feedback.

Percentages

Any kind of recognition is capable of acknowledging only a certain percentage of the company's employee population at any one time. It's important to be aware of this percentage to ensure that most of the employees can be recognized in some way at some time. Only two percent of Tennant's employees receive the formal Award of Excellence each year. If the remaining 98 percent were never recognized through day-to-day and informal means, there would be no viable recognition program at Tennant! Only full integration of **all three recognition dimensions** will allow the highest percentage of employees to be recognized.

Prestigious

If many employees perceive something as special or sought after, it is called prestigious recognition. Prestige can come through an article about the employee in the company newsletter, a dinner, or a commemorative award. The Award of Excellence is our most prestigious award.

Public Display

A public display makes recognition memorable because it puts the receiver in the spotlight. It sometimes includes a banquet or dinner, a formal presentation, and a tangible reminder. These events honor the recipients and highlight their achievements in front of peers and superiors alike. This high-visibility event is a powerful form of recognition.

Sincere

For recognition to be sincere it must be genuine. Sincerity may be demonstrated verbally or nonverbally, but it must be real, based on a foundation of trust and respect. Otherwise, it is meaningless.

Specific Feedback

To understand specific feedback, we should reflect on B. F. Skinner's concepts, which we outlined in the previous chapter.

Skinner said reinforcement should be specific and should incorporate as much information as possible. When someone is giving specific feedback he or she should be as precise as possible about the behavior that is preferred. Many of Ken Blanchard's seven steps for giving positive feedback highlight this specific approach:

1. Tell people you are going to praise them.
2. Praise people as soon as possible, otherwise the opportunity may slip away.
3. Tell people in specific terms what they did of value. This will make it easier for them to want to repeat the behavior.
4. Tell them how good you feel about what they did. Explain how it helped either you, their co-workers, or the company.
5. Pause. Let the message sink in.
6. Encourage a repeat performance of the behavior.
7. End with a smile, and possibly a handshake.[6]

We'll discuss more about specific feedback in Chapter 7.

Subjectivity

Since the reason for recognition is often in the eyes of the beholder, a certain amount of subjective judgment is part of the process. Generally, the more people involved in the selection process, even though they make their decisions based on objective data, the more dependent they are on the opinions and judgments of others.

From Superiors

Recognition from superiors means it comes from someone at a higher level in the organization. It may come from the employee's direct manager or supervisor, but not necessarily.

Tangible Reminder

A tangible reminder is something left behind to remind the person of the reason for the recognition. The size or monetary value of the reminder isn't as important as what it symbolizes. A note, certificate, pin, button, or mug is a constant reminder of the recognition. When the reminder is kept nearby, it helps keep the performance in mind. The recognition can be relived repeatedly.

Timely

Timely recognition means little time has elapsed between the action itself and the associated recognition.

Win/Win

When we talk about a win/win situation, we're describing a scenario in which everyone is a winner. There is no screening or selection process that eliminates anyone. At work, winners may be workers, supervisors, or managers. Recognition may also flow from supervisor to employee, from employee to supervisor, or between peers. Win/win may also describe an organization as a whole. A company where everyone is recognized is truly a win/win organization because everyone receives the benefit of recognition — and everyone feels good about it.

PUTTING IT ALL TOGETHER

At Tennant, we've devised a framework for defining formal, informal, and day-to-day recognition — the three types of recognition that comprise the company's recognition philosophy. We fit each of the values or attributes we've just described into a continuum, ranking each attribute in a low, medium, or high category in terms of its qualities. In this way, we create a picture of each type of recognition — its strengths, weaknesses, and how it best serves the organization's recognition goals. The continuum is useful in providing a quick grasp of the multiple

> *"Rewarding employees for their exceptional work is critical for keeping them motivated to continue to do their best."*
>
> **Ken Blanchard**[7]

attributes of each type of recognition. After looking at the continuums you can:

- determine your personal recognition preference
  and/or style;
- assess your organization's recognition climate;
- assess a specific recognition style;
- create the foundation for a new effort within your
  organization; or
- validate your own employee surveys.

As you examine the continuums for formal, informal, and
day-to-day recognition, keep in mind that the placement of an
attribute on the continuum — whether low, medium, or high —
isn't meant to assign a value on the type of recognition. It only
acknowledges the differences among the three.

FORMAL RECOGNITION

Formal recognition is a structured and defined
process that has a fairly even distribution of qualities.

LOW	MEDIUM	HIGH
frequent	from peers	consistent
interpersonal skills	subjective	cost
% of total	from superiors	prestigious
timely		public display
win/win		sincere
		specific feedback
		tangible reminder

Formal

Let's interpret formal recognition using this continuum,
beginning in the low column. Formal recognition ranks low in

frequency because formal recognition requires a long selection process and awards are given only one or two times a year. It is not **timely** for the same reasons. One may be recognized in December for something he or she achieved back in February. The **interpersonal skills** required to give formal recognition are also considered low. The CEO's formal award presentation at an annual banquet will most likely be a short prepared statement, not a personal chat. Finally, since few employees are recognized in the formal program, the **percentages** for formal recognition are generally low, a factor that ties in to the **win/win** attribute. A few employees "win" in a formal program, but many don't — so it may be perceived as win/lose.

In the medium category, we find that formal recognition sometimes comes **from peers**, sometimes **from superiors**. Its **subjectivity** also falls into the medium range. The multiple evaluations required in the formal process mean that many people are involved in evaluating a person's performance. More people means more subjectivity. However, this is offset by the precise and stringent criteria required for formal selection.

In the high column, we first find **consistency**, which means the process is the same every time. Formal recognition is also **costly**, a factor that is linked with its **prestige**, **public display**, and **tangible reminders**. Formal recognition is often made at a company banquet or special event. Guests are flown in for this event, and presented with jewelry, a company plaque, or other expensive gifts in the presence of company management. Formal recipients are recognized for specific achievement, which brings **specific feedback** into the High ranking. Of course, it is essential that the recognition be delivered **sincerely**.

INFORMAL RECOGNITION

Informal recognition is a non-structured, less well-defined type of recognition often used to single out groups

LOW ————————	MEDIUM ————————	————HIGH
subjective	cost	consistent
	frequent	sincere
	interpersonal skills	specific feedback
	from peers	from superiors
	% of total	
	prestigious	
	public display	
	tangible reminder	
	timely	
	win/win	

and teams as well as individuals. Its attributes fall mainly in the mid-range, as seen above.

Most of the attributes of informal recognition fall into the continuum's mid-range because there are fewer rules governing the process. In informal group recognition, a **win/win** situation is created for all team members. For both groups and individuals, there is the **prestige** of acknowledgement for your contribution to your department. Sometimes informal recognition is accompanied by a gift, sometimes not, therefore **cost** averages out. Sometimes there's a **tangible reminder** or a **public display**, other times not. Informal recognition may be **frequent** or **timely**, it may come **from peers**, or it may not. It does reach a larger **percentage of total** employees than formal recognition, and the **interpersonal skills** are more stringent than those needed for formal recognition.

Because of its specific goal-orientation, informal recognition ranks low in **subjectivity**.

On the high end, informal recognition is usually given to celebrate a particular goal or achievement as a **specific feedback**, and as such it is **consistently** applied. It almost always comes from a **superior**, and it should always be given **sincerely**.

DAY-TO-DAY

Day-to-day recognition is highly personalized, it's one-to-one, and attributes are polarized.

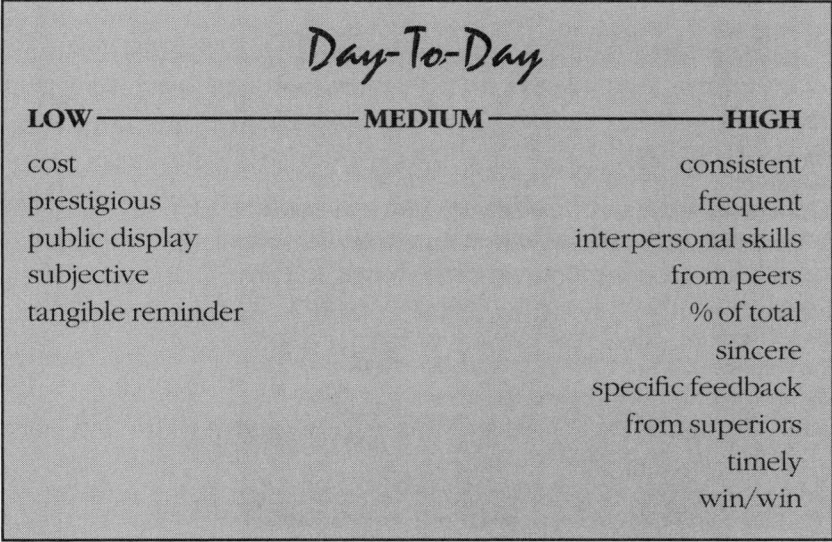

Day-To-Day

LOW ─────────────── MEDIUM ─────────────── HIGH

cost	consistent
prestigious	frequent
public display	interpersonal skills
subjective	from peers
tangible reminder	% of total
	sincere
	specific feedback
	from superiors
	timely
	win/win

Day-to-day recognition often **costs** nothing and leaves behind few **tangible reminders**. A pat on the back, a compliment, or a personal note are ways to recognize someone this way. Therefore, day-to-day recognition ranks low in **public display** and has little **prestige**. The person giving the feedback is the "judge and jury" for the recognition, thus taking away much of the feedback's **subjectivity**.

The giver and the receiver are both **winners** with day-to-day recognition, partially because the feedback is **sincere, specific, timely**, and is intended to be given **frequently** and **consistently** by **peers** and **superiors**.

While the return is high, the delivery of effective day-to-day recognition requires a high level of **interpersonal skills**, which may require prior training. Because this type of recognition goes directly from one person to another, and because most employees are receiving frequent and timely recognition, a large **percentage** of the total number of employees will receive recognition regularly.

A FINAL WORD ON ATTRIBUTES

Before we move to Chapter 5 and a thorough examination of formal recognition, here's a final word about attributes. It's important to realize that there is **no value judgment** regarding the low, medium, and high rankings of these attributes for the three types of recognition. In other words, if win/win ranks low in the formal process and high in the day-to-day process, this doesn't suggest that day-to-day recognition is better than formal. It is merely different. Each type of recognition has a unique combination of attributes. This emphasizes how important it is for an organization to provide a complete and well-rounded recognition program. A three-dimensional program, like the three-legged stool, is balanced and solid. A partial effort doesn't stand up.

If you examine the list of attributes closely, you'll see that only three of them — **sincere**, **specific**, and **consistent** — rank high on all three types of recognition. To successfully recognize someone, you must be as specific as possible. A general statement like, "You're doing a great job," is virtually meaningless because it conveys so little. It doesn't tell the person **what** he or she is doing that's so great, so that he or she can keep doing it. It also is insincere because it's a cliché. Recognition must be sincere to be meaningful to anyone. It must come from the heart. And it must happen the same way every time — consistency is essential for successful recognition.

"People respond to something that costs little or nothing, and that something is called recognition."

Edward Lawler,
Working Smart,
November 1990

Now let's dig into Tennant's first continuum — formal recognition.

Milliken & Company—
Non-financial Recognition

One of the champions of non-financial recognition is Milliken & Company of Spartanburg, South Carolina. Through its quality-oriented "Opportunity for Improvement" program, Milliken has embraced recognition as "the accelerator pedal for our vehicle of Quality," and they believe "the more we do, the faster we go."

Newt Hardie, former vice president of Quality, says Milliken avoids financial recognition since it can too easily take the place of face-to-face, verbal appreciation for work done. Instead, Milliken emphasizes non-financial recognition and the personal support of employees that goes along with it.

Milliken has found through a variety of recognition methods that they have created an environment where recognition is contagious. They stress that it is impossible to do too much when it comes to recognizing its employees — and for employees to recognize each other.

"Success breeds success."

❖

Tennant's democratic approach to recognition — to create a system of the people, by the people, and for the people — is designed for broad participation by employees.

Chapter 5

Tennant's Evolution — Formal First

Tennant's foray into the field of recognition began in 1981 as part of the company's quality improvement program. Phil Crosby's 14 steps toward quality had underscored the need for company-sponsored recognition, and many people were making outstanding contributions toward our quality goals. But Crosby did not include directions on how to accomplish recognition. The Corporate Quality Team, established to implement Crosby's 14 steps, was charged with the task of creating a recognition program. The team members knew only that we wanted to acknowledge employees' contributions to quality. They began by informally looking at the recognition programs of other companies. We found one trait we definitely wanted to avoid: a management group or an executive selecting award recipients. We believed this would make the awards seem biased to the other employees.

BEHAVIOR GOALS

Two years of research on recognition yielded a plan which we entitled "The Formal Quality Recognition Program." It established ideals or standards of excellence and recognized employees who, through specific work behaviors, conformed to those ideals. We also established three rules governing the selection of award recipients:

1. Our program would be peer driven. An employee could nominate anyone of higher, equal, or lesser rank, but not anyone he or she reported to directly.
2. Recognition recipients would be selected by a committee of employees of different rank and from different departments in the company.
3. We would establish criteria for selecting recognition recipients and print them on the nomination form.

To develop our recognition criteria, we asked ourselves what types of behavior would best achieve our quality goals. We came up with five. They became guidelines for judging individual performance in the areas of:

- customer expectations;
- work quality;
- interaction with others;
- initiative to solve problems; and
- support for Tennant's customer-focused quality emphasis.

FORMAL GROUP RECOGNITION

We also realized that some of the most striking examples of quality improvement at Tennant were the result of team effort. So we decided to include groups (both permanent and temporary), in our recognition program. A group, which could be as small as two people or as large as an entire department, also had to meet criteria to receive a formal award. Like the individual award, group recognition focused on long-term performance related to:

- customer expectations;
- work quality;

- interaction with others;
- initiative to solve problems; and
- ability to pursue and achieve objectives.

FORMING THE COMMITTEE

When we had established our concept and recognition criteria, we were ready to take the program to the people. John Davis, director of manufacturing engineering and product conformance and Tennant's quality effort mentor, asked eight Tennant employees from different areas of the company to form the first Formal Recognition Committee. "I chose committee members who were excited about the quality effort, had strong interpersonal skills, and showed a lot of initiative," says Davis. Though implementing the program was placed in the committee's hands, Davis stayed on call to guide the group.

THE TWO-PERCENT RULE

Since its inception, the Formal Quality Recognition Program has had as its centerpiece a prestigious award bestowed on an elite group of employees who have been employed at Tennant for at least one year and meet extremely high standards of performance. Individual awards are given to no more than two percent of Tennant's work force during a single year. Although two percent is the limit, that limit is rarely met because Tennant requires nominees to fulfill every one of the award's stringent criteria.

"One year, we could offer 32 awards based on work force percentages. But we only gave about 22 awards. We wanted to be sure we were giving awards for top-notch quality performance," says one committee member. "We established a minimum numerical score to qualify for each category. These standards allowed us to maintain the credibility of the program and the prestige of the award." Today the average number of individual recipients per year is 30.

Group recipients must also meet numerical standards. Any number of employees may make up a group, but Tennant's Group Quality Recognition Awards are limited to 12 groups per year. Of those, up to eight recipients are selected in the permanent group category and four among the temporary groups or project teams.

THE FIVE-STEP PROCESS OF FORMAL RECOGNITION

At Tennant, formal recognition in all categories goes through a five-step process: nomination, committee review, evaluation, selection, and banquet and awards.

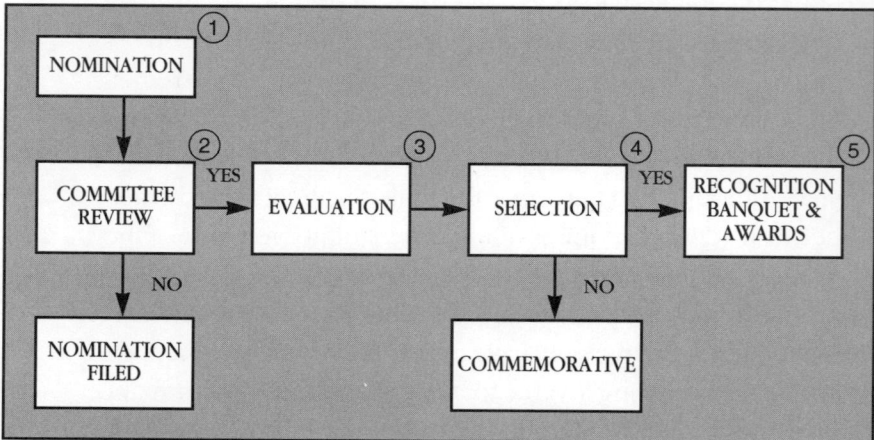

Step 1: Nomination

Tennant's democratic approach to recognition — to create a system of the people, by the people, and for the people — is designed for broad participation by employees. To encourage employees to nominate their co-workers, we made the process as easy as possible. Nomination forms are openly displayed in central locations throughout the company. And they're easy to use. A brochure describes the formal award's quality objectives, the selection criteria for individuals and groups, nomination deadlines, and instructions on where to send the form. Nominators are asked to name two customers and two co-workers who can provide supporting data on the person or group nominated.

> *"Receiving an award makes you feel good about yourself. It also feels good to know that my managers and my peer group thought I did a good enough job to receive a nomination."*
>
> **Award of Excellence Recipient**

The committee receives nominations for individual and group formal awards throughout the year. The committee acknowledges the receipt of a nomination with a thank-you note. This lets the nominator know the form has been received, acknowledges the person's efforts, and reminds the nominator of the timing involved. The deadline for individual nominations for a given year is December 31; recipients are chosen the following May. Group award recipients are chosen twice a year, in June and December.

Step 2: Committee Review

All individual and group formal award nominations are addressed to a special mail drop, then routed to the committee chairperson. After the deadline, the Recognition Committee meets to review and process the nominations. The committee first calls the nominee's manager or supervisor. If the manager approves the nomination, the committee forwards performance evaluation requests to the employees listed on the nomination form and to others familiar with the nominee's work. The committee sends evaluations to six possible evaluators, and it requires four completed evaluations from at least three different areas — co-workers, customers, and managers — to get a well-rounded view of the nominee's performance.

Step 3: Evaluation

Individuals contacted by the committee to evaluate the performance of a nominee are asked to complete a questionnaire and encouraged to include documents or data supporting the nomination. The process demands a serious commitment from the evaluators, who are required to provide specific and complete information. The evaluators are given two to three weeks to complete and return the form. The committee often conducts a follow-up to fill in information gaps.

Step 4: Selection

When supporting materials are received, the responses are reviewed by each member of the committee and numerically scored to reduce subjectivity.

The ranking system yields a list of nominees who meet the numerical requirements of the formal awards program — the top two percent. Finally, the committee takes a closer look at the people selected to determine which of them meet the award's highest standards.

Six weeks before the awards presentation, all nominees are informed of their nomination. Those not chosen to receive a Formal Quality Recognition Award are notified by letter, and invited to choose a commemorative gift. Award recipients are contacted by phone or a personal visit. They may also choose a commemorative gift, and are invited to the awards presentation.

Step 5: Recognition Banquet and Awards

Individual recipients of the Formal Quality Recognition Award are honored at a lavish banquet, held on the same day as the company's annual shareholders' meeting in May. Tennant President/CEO Roger Hale presents each recipient with the Award of Excellence, which is the Ring of Quality, a 10-carat gold and diamond ring modeled on the TQ™ (Tennant Quality) symbol.

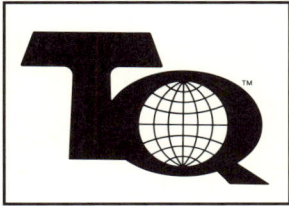

Recipients are also presented with a personalized Award of Excellence plaque. Second- or third-time recipients receive a 10-carat gold TQ pin accented with diamonds. Additional diamonds are added in subsequent years.

Attending the banquet are the award recipients, their guests, members of company management, and members of quality-related committees.

The big day begins with an introductory breakfast, followed by the shareholders' meeting and a formal luncheon. Out-of-town recipients are flown in and put up in a hotel the day before the celebration. Before the evening awards banquet, out-of-towners are given a tour of Tennant's Twin Cities facilities. For many people visiting company headquarters for the first time, this tour gives them their first broad perspective of their company.

The day after the banquet, visitors are given a tour of the city before returning to Tennant, where they meet their Twin Cities counterparts for a closer look at company operations. For example, a service person visiting from the field is matched with the service organization in Minneapolis for a day.

Formal recipients are featured in a special issue of the employee newsletter, *TENNANT TOPICS,* which includes a picture of all recipients and an article about their accomplishments. The names of recipients are also posted on Tennant bulletin boards and permanently engraved on a plaque in the reception area at our Minneapolis locations.

GROUP RECIPIENTS

As we've said, formal Quality Recognition for groups is given twice a year in two categories — one for permanent and one for temporary work groups. Unlike the individual awards, which are presented at company headquarters, the group awards are presented at a banquet in the recipients' region and hosted by the group's regional or department manager. In Minneapolis, all group recipients join together for one group banquet. The awards include the presentation of a 10-carat gold pin, featuring the TQ symbol, for each group member and a single Award of Excellence plaque for the entire group.

The Tennant welding department, described in Chapter 2, has set new standards for teamwork and efficiency and has received three formal group awards, an unmatched record to date. The third time they received the formal award, it was presented at a hotel in Minneapolis. Unbeknown to the welders, their supervisors had asked the restaurant staff to dress in the green fatigues that the welders wear at work. They enjoyed being waited on by people dressed in their own well-known uniform.

THE RECOGNITION TRANSITION

The first few years of our employee recognition program were marked by trial and error as employees familiarized themselves with the process and became comfortable with the recognition concept.

The early years also gave us the opportunity to see what worked and what didn't work. Before long we recognized a few glitches in our original concept and a few gaps that needed to be filled.

THE TWO-TIERED FORMAL SYSTEM

For example, the Formal Quality Recognition
Program, as we originally devised it, was a two-tiered system.
Though the program was geared toward recognizing the top two
percent of our employees, only about one-third of those people
received the top award.

The remaining two-thirds, who were nominated but did not
receive the Ring of Quality, received Special Recognition Awards
and were presented with a 10-carat gold pin featuring the company's TQ quality emblem.

"These individuals were top material, but they were in the
second level of recognition," said a committee member. "We had a
situation where somebody selected to receive one of the awards
felt like a loser because he/she received a Special Recognition
Award, instead of the Award of Excellence."

OTHER GLITCHES

The formal system tended to backfire for other
reasons as well. For example, many employees would look at a
recipient and question why that person was chosen to receive a
formal award. These critics were guided by their personal perceptions of the person and misunderstandings about why that person
instead of themselves was being recognized. Lack of knowledge
and jealousy may also have played a part. These factors led to dissatisfaction among some Tennant employees.

Other problems were caused by the lack of variety in the
company's recognition programs. In the early stages, there was no
system for informal recognition at Tennant. Also, the company
had yet to appreciate the importance of day-to-day recognition.

ADJUSTING AND GROWING

Overcoming these problems has been a process
of evolution. "We definitely did not start out with 1,800 people
fervent for recognition," says John Davis. "The transformation
developed slowly."

Some of the problems were overcome by communication.
By publicizing the accomplishments of individual and team recipients, rather than just publishing names and departments,
nonrecipients could better understand why an individual was
being recognized. Publishing this kind of information also pro-
moted and encouraged behavior that the company valued.

UPDATING FORMAL RECOGNITION FOR THE 1990s

In 1988, Tennant formed a 12-member steering committee to review the effectiveness of the company's communications. We surveyed 15 groups of Minneapolis and field employees
to determine the success of various programs. The 144 respondents identified recognition as a key issue, but the survey showed
that a few problems still existed.

In October 1989, the communication steering committee
recommended that Tennant abolish the two-tiered system of
recognition for individuals. The recommendation went into
effect in 1990.

The company has instituted other changes as well. Since the
Quality Improvement Process began in 1979, we have become
adept at achieving product specification quality. However, during
those years, we were meeting our own standards. Now we're
asking our customers to tell us what quality means to them. This
customer-oriented effort requires a new commitment to customer
service. It means we must recognize employees who achieve customer service excellence. Beginning in January 1992, Tennant
incorporated customer feedback into the performance criteria for

formal awards to reflect our 1990s emphasis on Customer-Focused Quality. To support this new customer focus, nominees are evaluated by their customers, as well as their supervisors and co-workers.

THE FORMAL RECOGNITION PROCESS TODAY

Today, as it always has, Tennant's Formal Recognition Committee contains a cross section of the entire company's employees — with representatives from each of the plants, and from manufacturing, engineering, and field operations.

Selecting award recipients demands a major commitment from the committee members, who put in about 100 hours a year. Between January and April, the committee meets for about two hours, two or three times a week, to read and process evaluations for the individual nominees, who are recognized in May, and for the first group recipients, who are recognized in June. Some lunch hours are devoted to meetings, but the committee's work cuts into the regular work day as well.

The committee is aware that people are recognized because someone took the time to nominate them. But nomination is just the first step. Every nominee must have supporting evaluations by co-workers, the nominee's manager, or customers. "If we could make one statement to employees," says past committee chairman Jeff Fliss, "we would tell them to fill out the evaluation as if they were the ones being nominated. It's sad when you realize that a deserving person won't receive an award because evaluations weren't returned."

One committee member recalled how she received the Special Recognition pin several years ago. She was working in the Accounts Payable Department and dealing with one of Tennant's suppliers. She found that the supplier had double-billed Tennant for an extra $25,000. To correct the error, she spent about 60 hours pulling together all the paperwork and working with the supplier to determine how to correct the error. The supporting documents that other employees wrote on her behalf, coupled with the substantial savings she had made for the company, helped her receive the award.

The committee's composition has changed over the years. Members have always had a two-year tenure, but early on, the entire committee changed every two years. In 1990, the committee shifted to a staggered-term system. Now, each year four new members are chosen, joining four experienced members. The change has helped maintain consistency in evaluating recognition nominations, and the four experienced members can help the new people organize and process the evaluations that come in soon after the membership changes.

As participation in the recognition process has grown, its driving force has shifted. "Nominations in the past used to be manager- or supervisor-driven. A manager would nominate someone in his or her department or someone in another area," says John Davis. "Today it's more peer-driven, and more employees are nominating their co-workers."

Davis's role in overseeing the program has also diminished through the years as employees embrace Tennant's recognition program. "In the last five or six years, it has become truly an employee-managed process," Davis says.

FORMAL COST

Tennant's two quality-related formal recognition programs consume the largest share of the funding for the company's recognition programs, running at about $60,000 annually — roughly $30 per employee per year.

Most of the costs associated with the program go toward the annual awards banquet, and the travel, hotel, and catering expenses associated with it. The awards themselves — the gold and diamond rings, pins, and plaques — are also costly items.

In addition, everyone nominated for a formal recognition award receives a commemorative gift. The gifts include coffee mugs and coasters, flashlights, pens, tool kits, and calculators, all with the TQ (Tennant Quality) logo. Recipients choose the gifts they want.

KOALA T. BEAR

Soon after Tennant's Formal Quality Recognition Program was underway, we realized that individual contributions to quality were too important and too numerous to be recognized only once or twice a year.

So in 1983, we created the Koala T. Bear Award, a monthly recognition program. To reinforce our emphasis on quality, we chose the koala bear as the award's namesake. The award was symbolized by a small, stuffed koala bear, wearing a Tennant Quality T-shirt.

Though the Koala T. Bear Award is lighthearted and fun, it is still considered a formal award by Tennant's standards. Recipients are selected through a written nomination process and must meet specific criteria. They are chosen on the basis of efforts in the areas of customer needs and customer-focused quality, relative to their job and project responsibilities. To receive the award, an employee must:

- exert extra effort to meet or exceed customer needs; or
- go above and beyond job requirements in a small group or special project; and
- consistently meet job standards and have a positive work attitude.

An employee can receive only one Koala T. Bear Award in a 12-month period; however, the number of Koala T. Bear recipients is unrestricted. Any number of employees may qualify for the award in any given month.

THE KOALA T. BEAR PROCESS

Employees are nominated for the Koala T. Bear Award by their peers or managers. The committee sends the nominator a thank you-note for taking the time to recognize someone for a job well done.

Eight Tennant employees from different ranks and departments serve on the Koala T. Bear Awards committee. Similar to the Formal Awards, the diversity of the committee ensures that at least one person knows the nominee or knows someone in the same work area who can evaluate the nominee's performance.

To get an accurate evaluation, the committee contacts people who benefit from the nominee's work. Evaluations can also come from outside the company — one employee was chosen for an award on the basis of a supplier's evaluation.

> *"The Koala T. Bear program gives people an ego boost. It makes them want to do a better job after they receive it."*
>
> **Ruth Utecht**
> **Koala T. Bear**
> **Committee Member**

CELEBRATION

Once a month, someone dons the company's Koala T. Bear suit and visits the recipient to present the award. Committee members and others gather around to honor the recipient while a committee member reads the list of comments which explains why the employee was nominated. The comments are vivid. "If you cut him he would bleed Tennant's corporate color —

blue/green," reads one proclamation. Another recipient is told, "You're like Radar O'Reilly because you can always predict what someone needs before they need it."

It's always fun to see someone getting the bear. It's like a Pied Piper with paws. "People see the bear walking down the hall and they know someone is going to get an award. So they fall in behind," said a committee member. As a result, a crowd is often on hand to see an award presentation.

Those who have already received one bear in the last 12 months and are nominated again receive a sticker to place on the original certificate. Some recipients have a lot of stickers. Others have as many as four bears.

PASSING THE "SNICKER TEST"

When it was first introduced, it seemed unlikely that the Koala T. Bear Award would pass the "snicker test." Tennant employees, asked for their perceptions of the new program in a formal written survey, felt that receiving an award from a person dressed as a koala bear was childish. So the committee dispensed with the costume, but kept the certificate and the stuffed koala bear. Once the costumed bear was eliminated, "Where's the bear?" was asked when the awards were presented. So back came the bear.

A lot of people have played the bear, including company president Roger Hale. But no one ever knows who is inside the costume. That's part of the fun.

THE BEAR TODAY

The Koala T. Bear Program is extremely popular at Tennant. After 10 years, its strength is reflected in the high level of participation among employees at all levels. On the average, the committee presents between seven and 10 awards each month.

Recently, the committee went to all three Minneapolis Tennant facilities to deliver a record 13 Koala T. Bears.

The list of gifts and prizes has also grown. Besides a visit from the bear, recipients nowadays are given a certificate, the stuffed koala bear, and a letter explaining their accomplishments. They also receive a bear pin and a bag of koala cookies.

Since Tennant brought back the bear costume, the only substantial change for this award has been in the committee structure, which like the formal recognition committee, has switched to a staggered two-year term that brings in four new committee members each year.

THE FUN FACTOR

Almost everyone has fun with the Koala T. Bear because of the surprise factor — few people realize they're about to receive it.

Two Tennant employees taunted each other for years with the prospect of a bear visit. "Comb your hair, Dennis," Steve would say, "they're on their way over here." Dennis would answer, "Steve, you'd better act surprised because they're coming back to see you." Every month they bantered back and forth — they talked about nominating each other, and nominating themselves. When the committee actually came to present one of them with an award, he thought it was a practical joke cooked up by his friend. But when the presenter read the first paragraph of the speech, he knew it was for real, and then he was speechless.

HOW DO EMPLOYEES FEEL ABOUT IT?

One committee member recalls getting her Koala T. Bear Award several years ago: "I was planning to leave early that day, but everyone kept saying, 'No, don't go, you can't leave.' I said, 'What's so important about me being here?' 'Joanne is going to get her Koala T. Bear today,' someone said. 'Well, I don't have to be here for Joanne's Koala T. Bear,' I said. They finally broke down and told me I was getting one too. I was so used to doing my job all the time, I didn't think other people noticed. But somebody did."

John Davis recalled how a Tennant employee, now almost 70 years old, received a Koala T. Bear a few years ago. He told John later that in all the years he'd been with Tennant, receiving that award was by far the most gratifying experience he'd ever had.

"People generally feel good when the person that sits next to them says, 'You do a good job and you deserve this bear.' It's a positive experience all the way around," said one recipient.

SERVICE AWARDS

Employees at Tennant are recognized formally for their length of service to the company. This is another long-term program. Presentation of the service awards for five- and ten-year employees is made by the employee's supervisor or department manager; 15-year employees are recognized by a Tennant vice president; and employees with 20 or more years of service are recognized by President Roger Hale.

SUGGESTION PROGRAM

Although Tennant prefers to focus on non-financial recognition, it continues to support its Suggestion Program, which was developed in 1946. The program awards cash bonuses to employees whose ideas save money for the company.

As part of the program, Tennant recognizes both tangible and intangible suggestions. For tangible savings, where a dollar amount can be calculated, Tennant pays 30 percent of the first year's savings, up to a cap of $15,000. Intangible suggestions, related to work safety, for example, are recognized with cash awards of $10 to $50.

When a suggestion is submitted, it is reviewed by the employee's supervisor, then passed on to an evaluator, who is the decision maker for the suggestion area. That person evaluates the idea thoroughly, using financial calculation and analysis, to determine if the suggestion is viable. For each initial evaluation they complete, evaluators receive a certificate, followed by stickers to add to the certificate. Other small gifts, such as pens and decks of cards, are also given, and two $15 checks are given monthly to evaluators whose names are randomly selected. More prestigious items such as watches and radios are given to honor-roll evaluators at an annual event.

The company recognizes with a certificate all employees who submit suggestions, whether an idea is accepted or not. "If people take the time to put their ideas down on paper, they deserve some recognition," says Jeff Fliss, who manages the program. Tennant also awards recognition certificates to those who submit ideas. Additional suggestions are acknowledged by adding Tennant light bulb stickers to the certificate. The company received 864 suggestions from 354 employees in 1991, an all-time high.

In general, Tennant accepts about 25 percent of the suggestions submitted during a year. When an idea is accepted and implemented, the employee or group who submitted it is presented with a check and a helium balloon, which calls attention to the achievement. "The money is just one aspect of it," says Fliss, adding, "We have some people that are more excited to get the ballon. People like everybody to know, 'hey, I did something.' The balloons often stay on display at workstations for a month." In addition, names of suggestion award recipients are spotlighted in each issue of *TENNANT TOPICS*.

A LOOK AT THE CHART

In the last chapter, we introduced the attributes of formal recognition and explained the needs they fill for employees. Those attributes were distributed like this:

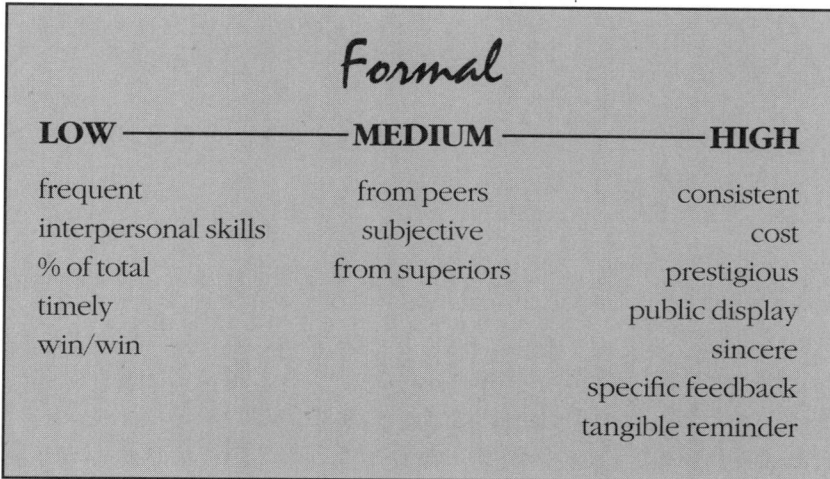

Formal

LOW	MEDIUM	HIGH
frequent	from peers	consistent
interpersonal skills	subjective	cost
% of total	from superiors	prestigious
timely		public display
win/win		sincere
		specific feedback
		tangible reminder

Our description of Tennant's two formal programs shows how they fill a need for employees. Both the Formal Quality Recognition Program and the Koala T. Bear Program are designed to consistently recognize specific behavior. Great pains are taken to provide valuable and tangible reminders of the recipient's achievements.

94

But formal recognition at Tennant doesn't fulfill every need, and can even cause problems, as we discovered early in our recognition journey. Most important, formally recognizing only two percent of Tennant's employees with the Individual Award of Excellence in a given year means that 98 percent don't receive an award. Some see this as a win/lose situation.

Also, the long selection process and infrequent award presentations weaken the link between the recognition and the superior performance it acknowledges.

Tennant Formal Recognition

AWARD OF EXCELLENCE	KOALA T. BEAR
5-step process	5-step process
groups and individuals	individuals only
began in 1982	began in 1983
elite - top 2%	no maximum number
5 guidelines	3 guidelines
committee	committee
evolutionary	evolutionary
yearly	monthly

Every September, *TENNANT TOPICS* features information and reminders about the formal recognition programs at Tennant to encourage people to participate. Information is given about all the different recognition committees and what they do. That gives people one last impetus to nominate peers for the Award of Excellence by the end of the year, and to keep Koala T. Bear nominations coming in.

Yet for all we get from formal recognition, we have to encourage other avenues as well. Our next chapter, on Tennant's informal recognition programs, will show one way we do just that.

HOW MANY RECEIVE FORMAL AWARDS?

From our employee base of about 1800, the number of Tennant employees receiving Formal Quality Recognition Awards has risen steadily over the years. The cumulative number of recipients of the formal awards are as follows:

FORMAL INDIVIDUAL QUALITY AWARDS
(Number of Recipients Cumulative)

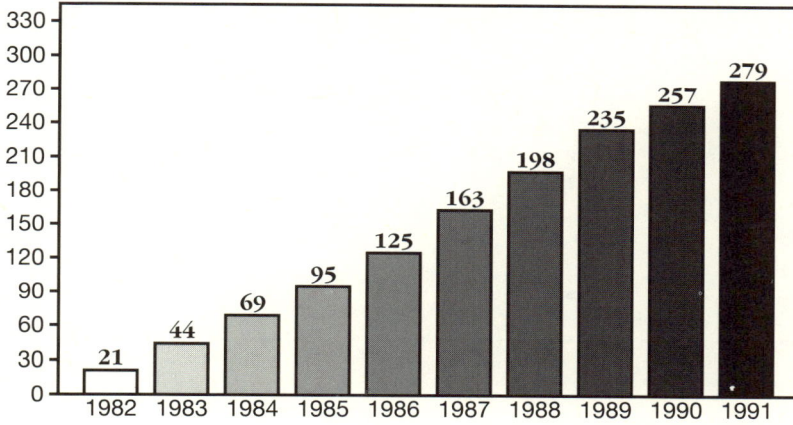

Year	Recipients
1982	21
1983	44
1984	69
1985	95
1986	125
1987	163
1988	198
1989	235
1990	257
1991	279

FORMAL GROUP QUALITY AWARDS
(Number of Recipients Cumulative)

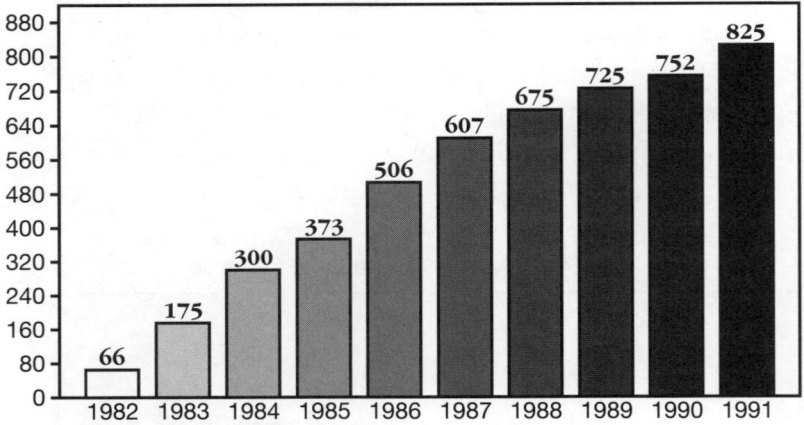

Totals 93 group awards for an average of 9 per year.

KOALA T. BEAR QUALITY AWARDS
(Number of Recipients Cumulative)

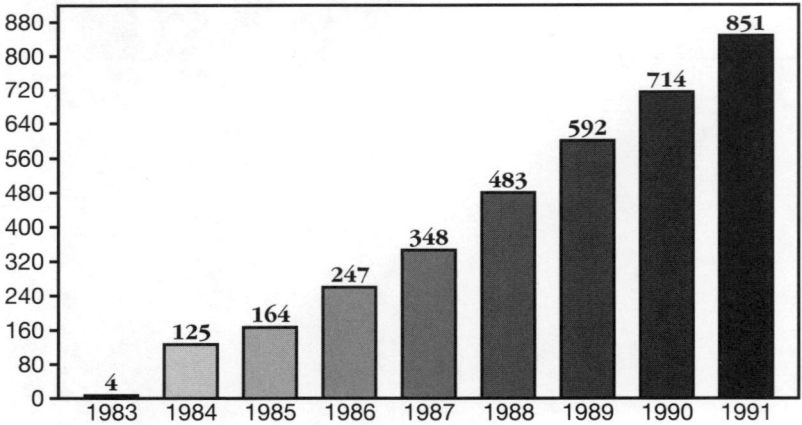

Awards begun in 1983.

GTE'S Formal Recognition

In its quest for quality, GTE, the fourth-largest publicly owned telecommunications company in the world, has been guided by an overriding goal — satisfying its customers. Recognizing those who meet or exceed customer expectations is the foundation of GTE Telephone Operations' formal recognition program, the President's Quality Awards.

"We share a dream at GTE to be recognized as the very best company when it comes to delivering value to customers, employees, shareholders, and communities. That's the foundation of who we are and what we do," says Kent B. Foster, president of GTE Telephone Operations. "Achieving that recognition is the key to our competitive edge, and the key to our profitable growth. Every quality award we present is further evidence that we're getting closer to fulfilling our dream."

The President's Quality Awards Program offers awards to recipients in four categories — Area and Region, individual employees, teams, and vendors.

GTE Telephone Operations' four areas and 14 regions compete each year for Quality Champion Cups. The award recipients are selected directly by customers surveyed annually. The most improved region is also recognized with a trophy.

Individual employees are recognized for excellence in customer service at three levels of achievement. The 10 top employees receive $2,500, along with a personalized award and a letter of commendation from the Telephone Operations president. The 30 finalists receive $750 and a personalized award, while the 40 semi-finalists receive $500 and a personalized award.

Each year, an individual is chosen from the ranks of the Individual Quality Champions to receive the President's Distinctive Commendation. The recipient of this prestigious recognition is a person who has demonstrated exemplary commitment to quality. He or she receives a monetary award, a special medallion, and a letter of commendation from the president.

Team awards are given to two first-place Gold Award winners (one for external and one for internal contributions to quality), two second-place Silver Award winners (one for external and one for internal contributions), three Bronze Award winners for external efforts, and three Bronze Award winners for internal efforts. Members of each team receive a cash gift, a personalized award, and letter of commendation from the president.

In 1987, GTE Telephone Operations expanded the scope of its formal recognition process with a Partners in Quality Program that rewards quality from its major suppliers. Those top vendors meeting the highest standards are recognized — along with the honored GTE employees — at the annual President's Quality Awards Program in Dallas.

Nominations for the President's Quality Awards come through numerous channels — from customers, peers, management, or in the case of the region awards, through customer survey data. After gathering data from local President's Quality Awards coordinators, nominations are reviewed by local committees and Area presidents. Top nominees are forwarded to the national headquarters executive committee for final selection.

All award winners, their guests, and select employees from each Area and Headquarters are brought to Dallas for a gala recognition event hosted by the Telephone Operations president and top GTE executives. Guests are met at the airport, checked into a Dallas hotel, and given a reception and dinner hosted by senior executives.

The following afternoon, nominees, their guests, and the select employees converge at the prestigious Morton H. Meyerson Symphony Center in downtown Dallas for a program modeled after Hollywood's Academy Awards, complete with a celebrity master of ceremonies, Dick Emberg, NBC sportscaster and GTE spokesperson. That evening, to culminate the festivities, there is a fabulous theme party honoring the winners. For all who attend, it is truly an event to remember.

❖

An event or a celebration can be a symbolically significant reminder of informal recognition.

Chapter 6

There's More "WE" than "I" in Informal Recognition

A manufacturer gives an award to departments that reduce job-related injuries.

A company executive presents gift certificates to employees who maintain a clean work environment.

A supervisor serves cake and punch to celebrate the completion of a major project.

The settings and circumstances of these three examples may differ, but they are bound by one common goal — recognition of groups of people who have done good work on the job. At Tennant, we call this Informal Recognition, and it is probably the most prevalent type of recognition found in companies today. But often the managers who use informal recognition do not realize that is what they are doing. For them, recognizing accomplishment is just part of the job.

INFORMAL RECOGNITION DEFINED

As we define it, informal recognition is used to recognize people who meet specific goals. Informal recognition occurs more often than formal recognition and less often than day-to-day recognition. It is flexible, and it can be tailored to meet the needs and preferences of individuals or groups. It can be given to individuals, though it is more generally given to a group.

At Tennant, departments, quality teams, cross-functional teams, and committees are recognized informally when they meet milestones, complete a mission, or achieve a specific goal. Individuals are informally recognized in our safety, name tag, and wellness programs, among others.

Along with formal and day-to-day recognition, informal recognition is one of the three dimensions of a complete recognition process. Though it may sound complex, it is easy to use.

HOW IT WORKS

Informal recognition is sometimes called random recognition, a term which describes one of the ways it can work. Finding someone doing something right — wearing a name tag, passing a random safety inspection, or demonstrating some other behavior encouraged by the company — often results in informal recognition. It is one of the best ways for an organization to say "thank you" for extra effort, reinforce a specific behavior, and provide an example to others.

TANGIBLE VS. SYMBOLIC VALUES

Recipients of informal recognition are often presented with a tangible item for their achievement. The dollar value varies from one organization to another. We have found that informal recognition is most effective when the item is more memorable than costly. An event, a celebration, or a small gift, like a T-shirt or coffee mug, can be a symbolically significant reminder of informal recognition.

The gift itself is not as important as the way it is given. The personal congratulations from the manager, the note or letter of recognition from a supervisor, or the phone call from top management that accompanies the gift is the focus of the recognition.

A LESSON IN CONSISTENCY

Before we implemented our Quality Improvement Process, most of us at Tennant were unaware of the importance of recognition, even though we had ongoing programs. "We had been using informal recognition for many years, although we didn't have structured guidelines," says Quality Services Manager Rita Maehling. "We knew that some groups were being recognized, but we didn't know what the distinctions were. We didn't know it was informal recognition."

For example, Tennant had a well-established informal recognition program for safety in the manufacturing area, but didn't have comparable efforts in other work areas. Employees in the non-manufacturing areas tended to say, "How come manufacturing gets hats and balloons and picnics, and we don't?"

We didn't really have an answer to that question. But we took it to heart when we implemented our quality process throughout the company. We quickly learned that good intentions are no substitute for a defined and structured plan. At that point, inconsistencies in our existing program began to undermine our efforts to provide quality recognition.

> *"Informal recognition helps people to feel part of a group. It empowers employees and groups so that they take action when necessary."*
>
> **Paul Brunelle**

Without guidelines, supervisors lacked direction on when informal recognition was appropriate, what type should be used, and how it should be administered. As a result, a number of problems arose.

For example, managers had been instructed to provide recognition for groups, but they didn't know how to do it. Some managers didn't know what type of behavior warranted recognition. Others were unsure of what to give employees. Some felt that they should not spend money for pizza parties and other "frivolous" celebrations.

As a result, managers informally recognized employees based on their own perceptions of what was appropriate. Some departments celebrated with pizza parties, lunches, and dinners on a regular basis. Employees in some departments received expensive baseball jackets, while other departments received nothing at all. Instead of improving morale or promoting productivity, these practices fostered jealousy and hurt feelings.

DEVISING A PLAN

In 1990, we took a major step toward solving these problems by establishing informal recognition guidelines for departments and small groups throughout the company. The guidelines gave managers the who, when, and how of informal recognition. For example, managers were encouraged to spend discretionary funds on a pizza party for a "recognized" group. This opportunity for informal recognition was a revelation for some managers and an affirmation for others.

GUIDELINES FOR INFORMAL RECOGNITION

By setting up guidelines, we tackled the problem that plagues many informal recognition programs — consistency — a problem often compounded by the diverse nature of the groups and the types of recognition they require. The criteria we developed, while not applicable for every organization, spelled out the basics: what kind of recognition was appropriate for what sorts of efforts; what the recognition was trying to accomplish; who was responsible for implementing it; and where the funding was coming from to pay for it.

Today, Tennant's informal recognition guidelines help managers and supervisors to more consistently implement an informal recognition system. Recognition depends on the:

> "*Without goal setting and measurement, a recognition program is fairly empty. You can't recognize people for performance if you don't know that the performance is good.*"
>
> **Paul Brunelle**

- amount of effort the group put into the project beyond the members' regular job responsibility;
- amount of time expended to accomplish the task;
- importance of the accomplishment to the entire organization; and
- ability of the group to set and meet goals.

Determining what type of recognition to give a group is the responsibility of the group's mentor or manager. This upper management support makes sure supervisors practice informal recognition regularly.

COST OF INFORMAL RECOGNITION

In a 1990 survey by *Potentials in Marketing* magazine,[1] one third of the 1,400 respondents said they budget between $10 and $24 for each item in their recognition programs, and approximately one fourth budget between $25 and $49. Although Tennant has no specified dollar amount for informal recognition, we believe we would fit closely into the range of this survey.

At Tennant, we set general guidelines to encourage informal recognition. Managers know that the achievement of a group or an individual mandates recognition, not a monetary payoff. If a department were to budget only $100 for group recognition, for example, and hold four $25 informal gatherings early in the year, it would have to ignore later achievements. That would not only undermine the recognition effort, it could destroy it. Consistency is the key.

TYPES OF INFORMAL RECOGNITION

There is no specific formula to determine the type of recognition appropriate for a given group. There are many different approaches. Building a plan for informal recognition requires real creativity.

At Tennant, we use various informal recognition tools. But they generally fall into a few broad categories:

- **Parties or Gatherings:** pizza parties, luncheons, or morning celebrations with coffee and rolls.
- **Outings:** tours of other companies, visits to customers or suppliers, or other off-site developmental activities.
- **Gifts and Give-Aways:** items such as coffee mugs, pens and pencils, or gift certificates.

The old saying, "The way to a person's heart is through his or her stomach," is right on target, at least at Tennant. Food is a popular way to celebrate accomplishments at this company. For example, members of our Zero Defects (ZD) Committee are given a dinner after successfully completing ZD Day. The dinner recognizes the committee members' long-term efforts in planning and hosting the event.

Three teams in the Tennant Assembly Department recently got together for a steak barbecue to celebrate bringing three Tennant product models "to audit." (This meant that a high percentage of machines coming off the line were assembled without defects, eliminating the need to rework the products before shipping.) The teams' managers cooked and served the steaks. Group photos were featured in the company newsletter.

Regardless of how it occurs, it is hoped that informal recognition at Tennant is also accompanied by a sincere "thank you," given verbally and in writing by the group's manager or mentor.

The options for informal recognition are almost infinite. The rule of thumb is "whatever fits, works." In other words, informal recognition should be shaped by the individual or group it intends to recognize.

EXTRA EFFORT TO PLEASE

Some Tennant managers go to great lengths to provide recognition that is memorable and fun. Eastern Region Operations Manager Nick Nicolay has invented memorable recognition methods that are uniquely tied to specific tasks. For example, to recognize a Tennant sales representative who had the highest level of reconditioned-machine sales, Nicolay shopped garage sales near his New Jersey home and found an old trophy. He had it reconditioned, and presented it to the salesman as a reminder of his achievement.

This personal approach is essential to Tennant employees working outside the corporate structure, says Nicolay. Many sales and service representatives operate out of their homes, some of them hundreds of miles from a company office. They get a boost from recognition, so Nicolay tries to make it special. "They don't get any reinforcement on a daily basis," he said, "so when they receive an award, they're overjoyed. That's what it's all about in my mind."

PERSONAL PREFERENCE — ROUNDING OUT THE THREE DIMENSIONS

Informal recognition also provides a sense of belonging for some employees. A Tennant assembly worker told John Davis one day that he had never belonged to an extracurricular organization during his school years, and wasn't currently active in anything in his community. "He'd been at Tennant for 12 years," says Davis, "and the small group activities and the recognition the groups had achieved were the closest thing he'd ever experienced to being a strong contributing member of a group. He wanted to tell me that it meant a lot to him."

FINGER ON THE PULSE

Informal recognition doesn't stand alone and it doesn't stand still. Situations and needs change. What works today won't necessarily work tomorrow. Therefore, it is essential to monitor employee reactions to the informal recognition programs being offered. Information coming through communication groups, or office or plant advisory boards, can give an accurate picture of how informal recognition is being practiced and received.

> *"An important part of recognition is that it lets people know the company sees them as individuals."*
>
> **Louise Quast**
> **Tennant**

In his research of nearly 1,500 employees, Dr. Gerald Graham, professor of management at Wichita State University and management consultant to the National Association for Management, found that the most common forms of recognition used by U.S. companies are often the least valued by employees.[2] These are the "holiday turkeys," the gifts given to everyone at the end of the year regardless of how hard they worked. This institutional approach runs counter to our approach, which is selective and specific. We believe that efforts- and results-oriented recognition makes a difference.

At Tennant, individual managers and supervisors are always trying to provide informal recognition that groups and individuals will appreciate. At the corporate level, we continually review the impact that informal recognition has had on the company. To improve the system, we survey employees to find out how frequently informal recognition is used and how it is received. We want to identify what works and what doesn't — so we can eliminate the ineffective areas, improve the others, and create new ways to recognize employees informally.

PART OF THE CULTURE

Informal recognition is an integral part of Tennant's culture today. "Who would have thought 14 years ago of inviting the president over for pizza and soda to celebrate the accomplishments of your small group?" asks John Davis. Today this is a normal occurrence. A commitment to the informal recognition process means that a production line can shut down for two hours to celebrate a group's achievement. Entire departments can go out to lunch at local restaurants. Gift certificates flow regularly to top performers in all areas of the company. Without the commitment of the entire company, such regular recognition would not occur.

> *"Recognition is now an accepted process at Tennant. It has transformed our company's culture."*
>
> **John Davis**

BOOSTING COMMUNICATION WITH NAME TAGS

One example of informal recognition sponsored by Tennant is administered by the Name Tag Committee. The program is meant to enhance employee communication and team spirit by randomly recognizing Tennant employees who wear their name tags on the job.

Once a month, the five-member committee meets to draw names of Tennant employees representing each Minneapolis facility. Members of the committee observe the employees to see if they are wearing name tags. The first two "tagged" people from each of four major Minneapolis work locations are chosen as that month's recipients. The committee then pays a surprise visit and says, "Congratulations. Thank you for wearing your name tag." They present each employee with a balloon and a $20 gift certificate; their names are posted on Tennant bulletin boards and featured in *TENNANT TOPICS*. After winning, the recipient's name is eliminated from the pool for a year, to guarantee that eight new employees will be recognized every month. "Tennant is a real people-oriented company, and we wanted to keep it that way by keeping communication open," says Committee Chairperson Carol Land.

The idea for the name tag committee, which began in 1983, grew out of Tennant's quality process. For many years Tennant had been a small company where everyone knew each other. "As the company grew," Land says, "that wasn't possible anymore. People would see others every day but wouldn't know their names." The management committee, searching for ways to improve communication, developed the name tag recognition idea as an outgrowth of reading *In Search of Excellence*, by Peters and Waterman.[3]

The program is very successful. Committee estimates show that 30 percent of employees consistently wore name tags in 1986. That average has doubled to 60 percent company-wide in 1991.

"It seems like a small thing," says Land, "but the impact is really great."

SAFETY PROGRAMS

One informal recognition program for safety began in 1975 to focus on prevention and provide continuous employee training on how to avoid accidents and injuries. It also offers cash awards to employees in departments that meet annual goals. To those departments that complete a year without a lost-time injury, Tennant gives each individual in the department $4. That cash award increases with each year — two years without a lost-time injury gives each employee $8, three years, $12.

As an additional financial award, Tennant pays another $4 per employee for every 100,000 consecutive hours worked without injuries. For example, if a department has gone 10 years without a lost-time injury, which amounts to 700,000 working hours, each employee receives $40 for the 10 years, plus $28 for the 700,000 hours, equaling $68 in cash for each person in the group.

Finally, many departments celebrate their safety achievement with a special dinner, a barbecue, or a small gift. A group photograph and story appear in *TENNANT TOPICS*. "It goes beyond the money," says Corporate Facilities and Risk Coordinator Louise Quast, who administers the program. "It means a lot to the recipients. They realize that people have taken the time to recognize what they've done."

The success of the program is undeniable. Tennant's workers' compensation rate is one of the lowest in the country, and several departments, including manufacturing departments, have gone more than 15 years without a lost-time injury.

This level of success has brought public recognition to Tennant for its safety efforts. The company has received a Minnesota Safety Council award every year since 1983 for "outstanding accident prevention performance in occupational safety."

In addition to the Safety Achievement Awards Program, Tennant has had an ongoing Safety/Housekeeping Contest since 1974. The goal of the contest is to reduce the number and severity of accidents, improve general housekeeping efforts, and increase safety awareness.

The contest is conducted over a period of several months. A Tennant Safety/Housekeeping inspection team, consisting of a management-office representative, an hourly person, and a manufacturing manager or supervisor, makes bi-weekly inspections to assess the level of housekeeping and cleanliness in the various manufacturing departments. Scores are tallied, and the departments' injury rates are also assessed. Each month of the contest period, one department is declared a winner, and every employee in the winning department receives a gift, such as a ceramic mug.

At the end of the contest period, prizes are given to the two departments that have the highest scores. Members of the top department receive an additional prize, such as a battery-operated clock radio.

The driving force for the contest is not the symbolic prizes. It is the friendly competition between departments and manufacturing facilities, and the positive interaction between hourly employees and supervisors during the inspection period. The result is real pride in the facilities, and a sense of camaraderie among the people who work in them.

WELLNESS PROGRAMS

Tennant's goal of promoting health and wellness is also supported by informal recognition. Under the guidance of the Wellness Committee, comprised of members from the entire company, employees are encouraged to take part in voluntary programs related to nutrition, exercise, mental heath, and other health-related subjects. The Pulse Program, for example, encourages employees to exercise. Registered employees keep track of their efforts and accumulate points. Their progress is displayed on company bulletin boards, and those who reach a certain point level receive gift certificates from the company. "Participation in this program keeps going up," says Committee Chairperson Linda Deml.

THE GROWING IMPORTANCE OF INFORMAL RECOGNITION

The variety of these programs and the amount of participation in them demonstrates the important niche informal recognition fills in our organization. An examination of current

> *"If recognition is done well, it reinforces the worth of an individual to the organization in a way that is meaningful and significant."*
>
> **John Davis**

trends shows that this niche is likely to expand at Tennant and in other organizations as well. Many companies today are adopting new management styles based on decentralization and are shifting toward a team-oriented work philosophy. More than ever before, employees seek personal satisfaction from their work, and that satisfaction can be enhanced by a variety of informal recognition. As a result, informal recognition is becoming more important than ever before.

"Teamwork leads to success," said Tom Peters in a 1990 *Working Woman* magazine article.[4] And teamwork and productivity are enhanced by attention to informal recognition. Why? Because it is an effective way to increase employee pride and morale within a group or department.

THE INFORMAL CONTINUUM

A review of the informal recognition continuum shows that most of its attributes fall into the medium range. It is less defined and structured than its formal counterpart, but more defined and structured than day-to-day recognition.

Since each informal situation is different, recognition attributes are broadly applied in informal recognition, so they average out in the middle. **Frequency**, **prestige**, **public display**, **timeliness**, **tangible reminders**, and a **win/win** situation all fall in the mid-range in relation to the other types of recognition. They are found more often than in formal recognition, but less often than in the day-to-day category.

Informal

LOW ——————————MEDIUM——————————HIGH

subjectivity	cost	consistent
	frequent	sincere
	interpersonal skills	specific
	from peers	from superiors
	% of total	
	prestigious	
	public display	
	tangible reminder	
	timely	
	win/win	

The **cost** of informal recognition is significantly lower than the cost of formal recognition, and can include a higher **percentage** of employees. A small group celebration over a pizza or a small gift to a group member costs considerably less than an annual banquet. The object of these informal celebrations is the successful accomplishment of a specific goal, and the party celebrates the team effort that made it happen. Instead of fostering competition, informal group recognition builds camaraderie among co-workers, a sense of being "in it together."

Although informal recognition can come from **peers**, it most often comes from **superiors**, who are usually responsible for initiating it. This places the attribute "from superiors" in the high range.

The manager's **interpersonal skills** must be well-developed to be effective in informal recognition because a small group in an intimate setting requires a personal approach, tailored to the recipients, not the broad statement used during formal recognition. However, informal recognition tends to be less demanding than the face-to-face communication required in day-to-day recognition.

Like formal and day-to-day recognition, informal recognition requires a highly **specific**, **consistent**, and **sincere** message. It is primarily goal-oriented, which makes the **subjectivity** rating of the recognition low.

In the next chapter, we'll examine the third dimension of a complete recognition system — day-to-day recognition.

Informal Recognition Tips

Management guru Ken Blanchard suggests a number of ways to informally recognize outstanding performers. None of these ideas carries a hefty price tag and some require only personal attention.

1. Write a letter to the employee's family telling them about the employee's recent accomplishment and what it means to you and the company.
2. Arrange for a top manager in your company to have a recognition lunch with the employee.
3. Set up a personal thank-you call from the company president.
4. Give the employee a small gift related to his or her personal hobby.
5. Give a pass for a three-day weekend to someone who has performed exceptionally.
6. Dedicate the parking space closest to the building entrance for the outstanding employee-of-the-month.
7. Wash the employee's car in the parking lot during lunch hour.
8. Personally make lunch or dinner for a small group of high performers.
9. Arrange to use employees in company commercials as AT&T and Ford Motor Company have done.[5]

❖

AT&T Network Systems

The Switching Systems Business Unit (SSBU) within AT&T Network Systems has a comprehensive, three-tiered integrated process for recognizing all contributions to quality within the Business Unit. The process is designed to build employee self-esteem, create an environment of mutual trust and respect, reinforce quality values, and motivate all employees to do their best to meet or exceed SSBU's business goals.

The Quality Recognition/Celebration Process covers day-to-day, informal, and formal recognition. The day-to-day process uses thank you notes, verbal recognition, calling people on the phone, or electronic mail. Informal recognition (cake and punch to announce accomplishments, a pizza party, dinner-for-two gift certificates) recognizes teams and individuals when they accomplish activities that meet or exceed quality expectations.

The formal process recognizes teams and individuals who meet or exceed a pre-defined set of criteria and contribute to the realization of the Switching Systems' goals. The SSBU believes that non-monetary recognition is more effective than cash, hence formal awards consist of personalized plaques or mementos.

Employees are encouraged to provide feedback and ideas to the Recognition Process Management Team to keep the program vital.[6]

❖

Chevron USA, Inc.

What could be more exciting than discovering a secret treasure? Chevron USA, Inc. employees who consistently exceed their job responsibilities through extra effort, problem-solving initiative, and teamwork have an opportunity to embark on just such an adventure.

The company's Treasure Chest is a fun, informal program that provides on-the-spot recognition to outstanding employees. The Treasure Chest is a large box, secured with a padlock, and brimming with all sorts of gifts. An employee being recognized is brought to the box by his or her supervisor, who holds the keys. The employee gets to choose an item, which may be a mug, pen, pencil, gift certificate, coupon for lunch or dinner, or movie tickets. Everyone loves a trip to the Treasure Chest.

A supervisor tracks the program by listing the recipient's name, what he or she did to receive the recognition, the name of the person selecting the recipient, and the item chosen. Recognition can come from supervisors and peers.

❖

Hartford Steam Boiler

The Hartford Steam Boiler Inspection and Insurance Company (HSB), an old and well-established company, implemented an informal recognition program in 1991 to recognize its administrative employees who meet four criteria:

* The employee is a team player;
* He or she takes initiative to solve problems;
* The employee provides leadership in supporting company goals; and
* He or she has an attitude that inspires other to do their best.

To recognize these individuals, the company spends up to $50 per year per employee and tailors gifts to employee interests. Recipients receive dinners for two, tickets to movies or sporting events, gift certificates, even coffee for a month. "I believe that when the final results are in, the investment will be returned to us many times over," says HSB spokesperson Karen Block.

❖

When delivered effectively, day-to-day recognition is a win/win situation for everyone involved.

Chapter 7

Day-to-Day Recognition

Day-to-day recognition, the third and final component of Tennant's recognition philosophy, is crucial to the success of any organization's recognition program. Like other forms, day-to-day recognition makes people feel good about themselves and their performance. It lets people know they are appreciated, that their work is important, and that others notice what they do.

People need day-to-day recognition to perform at consistently high levels. Although they can perform well without it, they probably won't want to. *In Performance Management: Improving Quality and Productivity Through Positive Reinforcement,* Aubrey Daniels said that performance problems are usually not "can't-do" problems, they are "won't-do" problems. "To identify a motivational problem, begin by asking the question: 'Could the individual do this job if his or her life depended on it?' If the answer is yes," said Daniels, "a motivational problem exists."[1]

Day-to-day recognition motivates people and meets an important human need. "People's need for positive reinforcement can be seen as similar to a business's need for profit," said Daniels. "A 'thank you' or other sign of appreciation keeps the individual's 'balance sheet' in check. It leads to an increase in morale, improves the quality of the work environment, and improves accountability."[2]

WHAT IS DAY-TO-DAY RECOGNITION?

A number of different terms can be used to describe day-to-day recognition. Some call it daily recognition. Others use the terms positive reinforcement or social reinforcement. At Tennant, we use the term **positive feedback** to describe this ongoing form of recognition.

Positive feedback is the verbal or written recognition that goes directly from one person to another. It can be as simple as saying "thank you" to someone you work with, or writing a short note that tells a person that you recognize the value of his or her contribution. Even a smile and a "good morning" to an employee is an acknowledging form of positive feedback.

WHAT DO PEOPLE THINK ABOUT IT?

The importance of positive feedback can't be denied, but it can be underestimated and overlooked.

A 1992 survey by Professional Secretaries International revealed that instead of receiving flowers or a luncheon, 30 percent of professional secretaries would prefer a simple letter of appreciation from their bosses. However, only seven percent of the respondents have received such letters.[3] The reason positive feedback is so often overlooked is inherent in its everyday nature. It isn't spectacular, doesn't cost a lot of money, but requires high levels of personal, heartfelt attention.

THE VALUE OF POSITIVE FEEDBACK

"Nothing is more important to a high performance organization than positive reinforcement," says Aubrey
Daniels. Daniels' management philosophy is based on the use of
positive feedback to change, improve, and reinforce performance
on the job.

Positive feedback's importance at work has been docu-
mented in numerous studies. Nancy Branton, project manager for
a 1989 rewards and recognition survey of the Minnesota Department of Natural Resources (DNR), found that recognition
contributed significantly to employees' job satisfaction. Most
responded that they highly valued day-to-day recognition from
their supervisors, peers, and team members. Sixty-eight percent of
DNR respondents said feeling that their work was appreciated by
others was important. The survey also revealed:

- 63 percent of respondents agreed that most people would
  like more recognition for their work;
- 67 percent agreed that most people need appreciation for
  their work; and
- Only 8 percent agreed that people should not look for praise
  for their work efforts.

"Recognition programs are more important now than in the
past," said Branton. "Employees increasingly believe that their job
satisfaction depends on acknowledgment of work performance as
well as on adequate salary. This is especially true of employees,
like those in the DNR, who are highly interested in their work and
take satisfaction in their achievements," she said.[4]

Positive feedback is appreciated by people at every level of
an organization. Tennant's Paul Brunelle recently recalled a conversation he had with the wife of a senior executive who was
accompanying her husband to an out-of-town conference. At one
point, the conversation shifted to recognition. The woman told
Brunelle that her husband wished he had received more positive

> *"Positive feedback is daily, ongoing recognition of people doing their jobs. It's nice to get appreciated for that."*
>
> **Marty Doering**
> **Positive Feedback**
> **Committee member**

feedback throughout his career. Her husband's bosses had not given him much feedback, she said, and he was starving for it. "That struck me," said Brunelle, "because the executive was a very self-assured, take-charge individual. I thought he didn't need to have someone say, 'good job.' But every person in the organization needs positive feedback, whether he or she is the president of the company, or someone who works in the office, the plant, or the field. Wherever you are, you still want positive feedback," said Brunelle. "It needs to go up, down, across, and in all directions in an organization. It has to be an important part of the culture."

IMMEDIACY COUNTS

The high value of day-to-day recognition is enhanced by its immediacy. Dr. Gerald Graham's research of 1,500 employees throughout the United States revealed that the type of reward most preferred by employees was personalized, "spur-of-the-moment recognition from their direct supervisors."[5]

SPECIFIC ATTENTION

Positive feedback has also been the focal point of studies by Kathryn Wall and Rosalind Jeffries, whose employee training work in the 1980s revealed an unmet need for employee recognition on a personal, day-to-day basis.

Their two years of qualitative research with 5,000 employees and managers from coast to coast showed that seven out of 10 employees at all levels said they wanted specific individual recognition for a job well done (see chart at right). Wall and Jeffries's

What Employees Want

*Qualitative research showed that **seven** out of **ten** employees at all levels said they wanted specific individual recognition for a job well done.*

"Recognition Secrets" seminar addresses the values and needs of today's work force and provides dozens of specific and practical recognition techniques. Their people-oriented approach focuses on individual, not organizational, attention. This is the core of positive feedback. "You have to catch people in the act of doing a good job," says Wall, "and acknowledge them individually and specifically for a job well done."

Wall and Jeffries have identified 70 simple, timely, specific, and cost-effective ways to give employees the personal recognition they need. The 70 items combine day-to-day recognition with incentive programs. "Employees are more receptive to formal, organization-wide programs if they believe that the company really cares about them on a personal day-to-day basis," said Jeffries in a 1990 *Training* magazine report.[6]

Day-to-day recognition is also the best way to honor people who are uncomfortable with the public display that happens in formal or group recognition programs.

SKINNER'S TOOL

As you might guess, positive feedback grew out of the behavioral studies of B.F. Skinner, whose work we examined in Chapter 3. In his experiments, Skinner discovered that the most effective reinforcement was both **immediate** and **specific** to the particular behavior. He also found that positive feedback was most effective when it recognized progress toward a goal rather than just the goal itself. Soon, Skinner was giving his subjects frequent small doses of feedback on an irregular and intermittent basis.

Skinner's technique — providing specific, immediate, spontaneous feedback from one person to another — is the basic model for providing positive feedback today. Sounds easy, doesn't it?

But it's not. Of the three types of recognition, positive feedback is the most difficult type to successfully implement and sustain. It requires a high level of interpersonal skill, an ongoing systematic approach, and the ability to recognize and overcome unconscious personal barriers in both giving and receiving. Telling someone, "I like what you did," is not easy for most of us. Saying it in the right way can be difficult too. First, let's examine how it should be done.

HOW TO GIVE DAY-TO-DAY RECOGNITION

In Chapter 4, we outlined the seven-step procedure developed by Ken Blanchard for praising someone properly. To summarize:
1. Tell the person that you intend to praise him or her.
2. Give praise as soon as possible.
3. Tell people specifically what they did that was outstanding.
4. Tell people how good you feel about what they did, and how it helped you, their co-workers, and the organization.
5. After you've praised someone, pause and let the message sink in.
6. Encourage the person to repeat the performance.
7. End the encounter with a smile and possibly a handshake.[7]

A FEW MORE POINTERS

Though these are the basic rules for giving positive feedback, there are a few other pointers that may help you get your message across.
- It's important to choose the right time and place to give positive feedback. If it's your first meeting with someone, your best bet is to have the conversation in private. Call the person into your office when he or she is alone in the hall. Save a "public display" for the formal award program.

- Make eye contact with the person you're complimenting. You want to make people comfortable and you want to convey your sincerity.
- Use the person's first name, if possible — it's more friendly.
- Keep it short and simple. Say it your own way. Positive feedback doesn't require a lot of flowery language or long explanations. It is meant to personally recognize someone by conveying the message, "The report was clearly written and covered all of the issues — and I want you to know that you did a great job on it."

WHEN TO GIVE POSITIVE FEEDBACK

Ideally, people should be given positive feedback whenever their work meets **or** exceeds expectations, as well as for small, incremental gains. Although that's not always possible, if you are aware and committed to the process, you can learn to regularly give others the positive feedback they deserve. Keep in mind that it is a learning process, and that you'll improve with practice. Give positive feedback:

- When it is deserved;
- When the person knows you are in a position to know it is deserved;
- When you know you are doing it for the other person's benefit — not your own; and
- When you want to do it.

Giving positive feedback can seem risky. Maybe the person will suspect your motives. Maybe the conversation will be awkward or uncomfortable. Whatever your doubts, one thing is certain — when it comes to positive feedback, trust and credibility are established through effective practice. Not only do you get better at giving positive feedback, but people get better at receiving it. After a while, they'll probably start giving it back to you.

GIVING AND RECEIVING POSITIVE FEEDBACK

Difficulties sometimes arise simply because of
personalities. Most of us know the adage, "some people are ruled
by their hearts and others by their heads." This statement
describes two personality types. Although each of us is unique,
we do tend to fall into certain personality profiles developed by
social scientists to predict and understand our behavior.

The Myers-Briggs personality typology, one such model of
personality types, indicates that with many managers, supervisors,
and executives, "thinking and judging" qualities dominate over
"feeling and perceiving" qualities. Unfortunately, people with
dominant "thinking and judging" personalities often have trouble
giving **and** receiving positive feedback. The characteristics that
drive them up the ladder of success aren't the same ones needed
to be in touch with providing positive feedback.

BARRIERS TO GIVING POSITIVE FEEDBACK

Some "thinking-judging" types can be resis-
tant to the idea of positive feedback. Based on past experience,
they've formed opinions about work, relationships, and expectations. Some of the attitudes that are common barriers to positive
feedback might be:

- I came up through the ranks without receiving positive feedback, and I don't see why everybody can't do the same;
- I think that positive feedback will foster complacency in the
  recipient — that it will go to someone's head; or
- I feel that a certain level of performance is expected as part
  of the job, and the paycheck is thanks enough for the effort
  the employee has given.

The first two attitudes are examples of the "boot camp" men-
tality that typifies many hierarchical organizations. The second

and third also highlight the erroneous belief that providing recognition will cause standards to slide and performance to drop.

On the contrary, positive feedback, like other forms of recognition, is more than a way to make everyone feel good (although it does have that beneficial effect). It is meant to acknowledge good performance. Given consistently, it encourages, reinforces, and motivates people to achieve consistent top performance. Ultimately, it can improve performance across the board.

MIXED MESSAGES

Some people have every intention of giving positive feedback, but they deliver it ineffectively — and undermine or destroy the message.

Giving mixed messages — mixing negative and positive messages — is a common problem in delivering positive feedback. When someone says, "You did a wonderful job on that report, John. It was very thorough. But it shouldn't have taken so long. I should have had it yesterday," the person is delivering a mixed message. The recipient will only remember the negative response.

The "great job, but..." approach takes other forms as well. Some mixed messages are offered sandwich-style — a nice remark to start things off, followed by criticism, followed by another positive statement. The person giving the message may think the approach comes out as positive. But in reality, the criticism sours the whole message.

Another type of mixed message occurs when positive feedback is used as a lead-in to another subject. Even if it is non-critical, this change of focus makes the positive feedback seem insincere. The recipient feels set up. The positive feedback becomes flattery to soften the person up, and manipulate him or her into working harder or taking on a disagreeable job. The recipient detects an ulterior motive when a manager says, "Julie, that was a dynamite presentation you gave this morning...By the way, I'm running behind on a project and could you..."

Remember, positive feedback cannot be conveyed through mixed messages. They undermine trust and are worse than nothing at all.

THE FOUR-TO-ONE RATIO

A reprimand carries much more impact than a compliment, says Ken Blanchard, who has extensively researched people's perceptions of praise and criticism. Blanchard follows Aubrey Daniels's formula: that for every negative interaction a person receives, four positive interactions are necessary to offset it. A statement offering both praise and criticism will be perceived as a negative statement. Those who want to provide positive feedback should keep this four-to-one ratio in mind. Giving praise and criticism in equal amounts does not balance out — it is generally perceived as negative or unfair. To be appreciated, positive feedback must stand alone, and positive statements must outnumber negative ones by at least four to one.

WAITING TOO LONG

As we have said, positive feedback must be delivered promptly if it is to be effective. Its impact diminishes if it is delayed. Studies show that the most effective way to reinforce someone is while a behavior is occurring. However, that's not always easy to do.

One way to meet this need is by the MBWA approach —

"management by walking around." Many companies, including Tennant, have adopted this technique so that managers are exposed to situations where they can give positive feedback. Managers don't walk the shop floor looking for problems, they focus on catching people doing something right and recognizing them for it on the spot. "At Tennant we push ourselves to get out and talk to as many employees as we can," said Paul Brunelle, who has served as mentor to the Positive Feedback Committee since 1987. "It's a very powerful type of recognition."

AVOID THE IMPERSONAL

As we discussed in Chapter 1, recognition is a good way to build self-esteem, and positive feedback helps build the foundation. In a family, parents use positive feedback to help their children develop healthy feelings about themselves and their personal worth. The same feedback is needed by adults to reinforce their value at work.

In her book, *I Saw What You Did & I Know Who You Are*, performance management consultant Janis Allen outlines some "don'ts" for giving positive feedback. To summarize:

- Don't ask someone to do your reinforcing for you. Sometimes a company president writes a standard letter, has a mountain of them printed, and instructs supervisors to pass them along to employees to "congratulate them for their work." The letters are passed out in a meeting with a comment like, "The big boss wrote this letter and told me to give it to you." This is not very inspiring.
- Don't give someone positive feedback from "the company." Some people try to give positive feedback by saying, "Good job. The company appreciates it." But the company is an abstract concept, not a person, so the recognition is meaningless. Positive feedback must be personal. That means it must come from a person.

HOW TO RECEIVE IT

Unlike giving positive feedback, which requires practiced interpersonal skills, receiving positive feedback is a less complicated matter — at least it should be. Simply look at the person complimenting you, listen to the message, and say, "Thank you." Accept the praise, let it energize you. You are being appreciated and noticed. Nothing but a thank you is required. With practice, recipients of positive feedback learn to accept recognition and then pass the recognition on to others.

We've already seen how difficult it is for many of us to give positive feedback, and for some people, it's also hard to receive it. Let's see why.

Receiving helps to perpetuate the cycle.

Effective receiving +

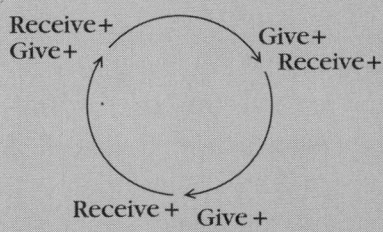

Receive +
Give +

Give +
Receive +

Receive + Give +

Cycle is perpetuated.

Ineffective receiving –

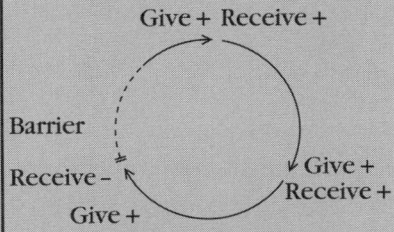

Give + Receive +

Barrier

Give +
Receive +

Receive –

Give +

Cycle is broken.

BARRIERS TO RECEIVING POSITIVE FEEDBACK

Have you ever praised someone's work only to have them reply, "Oh, it was nothing," or "Everyone else did the work"? Or maybe the person makes a joke out of it by saying, "Yeah, quite a change for me, huh?"

These responses — dismissing, disclaiming responsibility, or joking — are the three most common barriers to receiving positive feedback.

Some people can't accept positive feedback simply because they haven't had much experience receiving it. When they were children, their parents may have withheld praise and recognition to avoid spoiling them or to foster self-reliance. Instead, they fostered low self-esteem.

For many of these people, no achievement, however noteworthy, was noticed or acknowledged. As a result, many of them grew up striving for perfection and thinking that nothing they did was good enough. Since they never achieve perfection in their own eyes, they find positive feedback very difficult to accept.

Other people were not only denied positive feedback, they grew up surrounded by negative reinforcement. These people probably learned to perform only to avoid disapproval or some other negative attention. They aren't comfortable being noticed at all, even to accept a compliment. They keep waiting for the ax to fall.

Recognizing someone with low self-esteem or a history of negative reinforcement can sometimes provoke anxious or fearful reactions, which may come across as brusque or even hostile behavior. Being confronted with these reactions can make a person wary of giving positive feedback a second time.

But don't give up, and don't take rejection personally. These reactions are usually attempts to mask discomfort, so try to find a way to give these people the recognition they deserve in a non-threatening way. Perhaps the person would be more comfortable with a written message instead of a face-to-face encounter. Then the person can enjoy it privately without being put on the spot. Given time and practice, people with low self-esteem can learn to enjoy positive feedback.

MIXING TANGIBLE REWARDS WITH POSITIVE FEEDBACK

Sometimes problems crop up because, as Janis Allen says, "I sent a circle, but you received a square." In other words, the person is making a sincere effort to reinforce someone, but the receiver doesn't interpret it that way.

That's often the problem with institutional forms of reinforcement, such as the standard coffee mug or cash rewards. "This is all they think I'm worth?" the recipient thinks as someone hands him or her a $10 gift certificate.

As we discussed in Chapter 4, the problem with tangible rewards is that their value can be misunderstood. Rather than the tangible item symbolizing the accomplishment, it's taken at face value. Suddenly, the accomplishment is equal to the $10 gift certificate or the cost of a T-shirt.

Often it's easier for a manager to hand someone a T-shirt than to express appreciation. If the tangible is stressed, instead of heartfelt appreciation, the recognition can seem to be cheap.

When it comes to balancing tangible recognition with positive feedback, Allen suggests using another four-to-one rule. A person should get four verbal recognitions for every tangible one. Then the tangible item becomes a reminder of the positive experience of recognition.

POSITIVE FEEDBACK AT TENNANT

Late in 1983, Tennant's Operations Committee, which consists of members of upper management, made positive feedback a priority. We hired a consultant to help us develop a plan for this third dimension of recognition. The following year, we set up the Positive Feedback Committee to integrate the plan into Tennant. The committee's mission is to:

- enjoy working together;
- look for positives;
- understand and appreciate each other;
- build each other's self-esteem; and
- handle negative situations in a positive way.

Since then, the company has made a continuous effort to implement daily positive feedback. We began by training all employees. Although they really took it to heart, Tennant employees revealed in random surveys that our recognition efforts were still too few and far between.

As it turned out, perceptions of the level of positive feedback varied depending on a person's vantage point. Supervisors felt they were giving a lot of positive feedback, but many employees felt they seldom or never received it. When we examined these responses, we realized that a supervisor, who might manage up to 15 people, might give positive feedback to three people a day. For the supervisor, that seemed like a lot of attention. But that meant 12 people were not receiving feedback.

> *"People should feel good about them-selves — everybody should get a few positive strokes. You can't make anybody have self-esteem, but sending out positive messages might help."*
>
> **Rudy Holzinger**
> **Positive Feedback**
> **Committee member**

"We had to make people aware that positive feedback can move laterally, between co-workers," says one committee member. That required a basic cultural change at Tennant. Our long-term goal was to integrate positive feedback throughout the company.

Affecting that cultural change has been the work of the Positive Feedback Committee. This nine-member committee, made up of Tennant employees from all levels of the company, constantly strives to keep positive feedback at the top of everyone's mind. By stressing the importance of daily positive feedback, the committee encourages employees to participate in a two-way process of giving and receiving. "We try to make sure that the tools are there," says a committee member. "They make it easy for everyone to give positive feedback."

Janis Allen likes to recount a story that illustrates how people whose "cup runneth over" with positive feelings often learn to pass it on to others:

A consultant received a packet of course materials in advance of a class he was to take, requesting that he complete some preliminary work by the first course session. Along with the request, the instructor said that he would recognize any student's efforts to prepare for the course.

When he arrived at the class, the consultant found that the instructor gave M&M candies to each person who demonstrated knowledge of the material. By late morning, each student had accumulated a large pile of M&M's®.

About two hours into the course, after receiving steady reinforcement, students began rewarding each other with M&M's. "When people accumulate enough reinforcement, they feel comfortable giving it to others," says Allen. It also shows that when people get reinforcement from their peers they realize how important it is. "They discover a whole new dimension of recognition and reinforcement," says Allen.[8]

SPELLING IT OUT

One of Tennant's most effective tools for giving positive feedback is the That-A-Way note. A simple note pad introduced in 1984, That-A-Ways provide a quick and convenient way for managers and peers to give timely and specific written positive feedback. Today, That-A-Ways are a widely used tool at Tennant for two major reasons:

First, some people are uncomfortable praising a person face-to-face. While instruction and skill-building may alleviate some of the anxiety, the fact is, some people are uncomfortable — it's not their style. For those people, writing a That-A-Way note is a more appropriate way to provide positive feedback.

Second, people love to receive That-A-Ways. The notes provide a memorable token of recognition which can be savored long after the recognition is past.

Walking through the halls at Tennant, one will see bright yellow That-A-Ways posted everywhere. Some people have covered walls or bulletin boards with them. Other people display their That-A-Ways on their desk-tops under glass. "People like That-A-Ways," said one committee member. "It's one of the most

---

"THAT–A–WAY"

TO: _Chris_

Great job on your budget forecasting and for all the help you did to prepare for our meeting. The council was impressed with your numbers — I was impressed, too!

Lynn

---

well-accepted forms of recognition because anybody can do it."
"When you get one of these positive feedback notes," said
another, "you have a feeling that it is genuine and sincere, because
the person wouldn't take the time to write it unless he or she really
meant it."

Even groups receive That-A-Ways. For ZD (Zero Defects)
Day, the Positive Feedback Committee created a huge That-A-Way
for the ZD Planning Committee to recognize them for organizing
the all-day event. Literally hundreds of Minneapolis Tennant
employees signed the wall-sized note. The committee also sends
over-sized That-A-Ways to departments that win safety awards.

In 1991, the Positive Feedback Committee expanded the
That-A-Way note program by creating a wider variety of That-A-
Way note pads, including pre-printed notes and stickers. The
committee also gathers information on top performers to feature
in a That-A-Way page in *TENNANT TOPICS*.

The committee maintains Tennant's awareness of positive
feedback through a number of other programs and activities. For
example, the committee holds informal get-togethers for employees during the year. Every year, the committee sponsors a Positive
Feedback Day. On that day, Tennant employees are met at the
door beginning at 6:00 a.m. with That-A-Way note pads, pens
printed with the phrase "Positive Strokes Only," balloons, and
signs. At holiday time, the committee sponsors an open house
with cider and cookies and invites employees to drop by at sched-
uled breaks.

In addition to these programs, the company has developed
videos, posters, buttons, magnets, stickers, and positive feedback
mission cards to spread the word. President Roger Hale has
stressed the importance of positive feedback in his "President's
Corner" articles in *TENNANT TOPICS*, and the Positive Feedback
Committee has set up a booth at company-wide Zero Defects
(ZD) Day celebrations. Tennant has also taped internal round-
table discussions on positive feedback to present to Tennant

departments. Also, in 1990, positive feedback was added to our performance evaluation form.

GETTING IT RIGHT...IN THE FACE

Dr. Negative, a zany character played by Tennant employee Rudy Holzinger, helped spread the positive feedback message throughout Tennant from 1986 to 1990. Dr. Negative was introduced in a videotape training series to teach employees how to give effective positive feedback. In the video, Dr. Negative gets a pie in the face every time he gives a mixed message instead of positive feedback. The tape is hilarious and gets the message across at the same time.

Dr. Negative was so popular that the following year the company introduced Professor Positive, Dr. Negative's alter-ego, to the training program. The two characters have also appeared on Tennant posters.

OVERCOMING BARRIERS

In a 1991 article in *Quality Progress,* quality consultants and authors Donald L. McLaurin and Shareen Bell emphasized that improving communication skills within an organization is necessary to achieve quality. "When we talk about cultural change, what we usually mean is behavioral change, both for the individual and the organization," they said. "Such behavioral change doesn't come easily or naturally for most of us. To change, we must use skills that many of us lack but that all of us can learn."[9]

This philosophy is the foundation of Tennant's training effort. Tennant has conducted regular company-wide employee training and skill-building programs in two areas: communication skills and recognition.

In the 1980s, communication training at Tennant focused on one-on-one interpersonal communication. It was intensely skills-oriented, stressing active listening and communicating clearly and specifically.

"Listening may seem like a commonplace skill, but I've found it is neither valued nor practiced nearly as much as it needs to be," said Ken Blanchard in a recent issue of *Quality Digest*.[10] In Tennant's program, participants learned techniques to improve their listening skills by listening more frequently, systematically, and, as Tom Peters says, naively. Participants learned to ask open-ended questions, restate what someone says using that person's own words, and other techniques to achieve common understanding.

In 1990, all managers, supervisors, and lead individuals received Tennant's three-dimensional recognition training. They learned the importance of recognition and how to deliver it effectively. The ongoing course stresses the importance of positive feedback and teaches the participants techniques for providing it effectively. In 1991, this training was made available to all Tennant employees.

PROGRESS OF POSITIVE FEEDBACK

In becoming an organization that thrives on positive feedback, Tennant's culture has changed. It has taken time, patience, and persistence, but it is paying off. Today, positive feedback travels not only from the top down, but in all directions. It is here to stay.

Three surveys, conducted in mid-1984, late 1984, and again in 1987, showed that positive feedback had become an integral part of the company and was continuing to increase in importance. Tennant's communication and recognition training has helped keep things moving in the right direction. In addition, the company has integrated ongoing communication into daily operations. Managers and supervisors meet together monthly to keep channels of communication open, solve problems, and work on communications issues. They also hold monthly departmental meetings to improve communication throughout the company.

There's always room for improvement in giving and receiving positive feedback. Recognizing this, Tennant monitors its progress periodically. The surveys mentioned above are one way we keep tabs on our progress. In 1987, for example, Tennant developed a self-scoring assessment to help individuals assess their attitudes toward positive feedback and determine their own level of positive feedback frequency, skill, and awareness. Finally, adding positive feedback to the performance appraisal system helps make awareness a high priority.

Plans are under consideration to conduct employee attitude surveys every two to three years, beginning in 1993, to measure our progress in positive feedback at Tennant.

THE DAY-TO-DAY CONTINUUM

Unlike informal recognition, in which most attributes collect in the middle of the recognition continuum, the attributes of day-to-day recognition are positioned on either end.

Like the other two forms, day-to-day recognition is highly **consistent**, **specific**, and **sincere**. Since it is designed to be an ongoing means of recognizing performance, positive feedback is also very **frequent** and **timely**. It goes directly from one person to another, **from peers** or **superiors** alike. Its one-on-one style requires the highest level of **interpersonal skills**, which must be supported through employee training and skill-building programs. When delivered effectively, day-to-day recognition is a **win/win** situation for everyone involved. It enables the largest **percentage of employees** to feel good about their performance, and it is a boost for the person giving the recognition.

Saying thank you costs nothing. And writing a note of appreciation costs nothing in dollars and very little in time. For that reason, its **cost** ranking is low. Its **prestige**, **public display**, and **tangible reminders** rankings are also low. Finally, day-to-day recognition ranks low in **subjectivity** because it acknowledges a person's specific performance.

Now that we've examined the three dimensions of recognition, we'll help you assess your current situation and set goals for getting where you want to go.

Goulds Pumps, Inc.

For Goulds Pumps, Inc., based in Seneca Falls, New York, day-to-day recognition is the foundation of the company's Total Quality Program. Guided by a nine-member recognition committee, the company's Water Technologies Group has pulled together an array of recognition tools — including a Recognition Plan book, logo, posters, notepads, and Recognition Awareness Boards to boost the use of day-to-day recognition among production and office employees.

"Recognition is one of the cornerstones of a Total Quality environment," said Group Vice President Frank Zonarich. "If you recognize people for the excellent work they do, you'll motivate them to continue working in a quality way."

The company began its recognition effort in 1990 by creating a 12-point recognition policy. The policy tied recognition to the company's Total Quality Principles which make recognition the result of top performance. Goulds's policy also stipulated the use of symbolic, non-monetary recognition.

The company followed up with field research, observation of Tennant Company's recognition approach, and a written Recognition Plan. "Tennant recommended building a solid base of day-to-day recognition. And that's the approach we took," said Manager of Advertising and Sales Promotion Jim Flanders, who helped develop the program.

The results have been excellent. In a survey sent to Goulds's employees in November 1990, 91 percent of respondents felt that being recognized is very important to their job satisfaction. And 73 percent of field sales and warehouse respondents felt that they received good or OK recognition from their supervisors. Sixty-eight percent of office employees rated their supervisors good or OK, and 57 percent of plant employees rated their supervisors at that level.

❖

Recognition puts everyone on the same team reaching for the same goal — success.

Chapter 8

Putting It All Together

We've now examined Tennant's three-dimensional recognition model, including the formal, informal, and day-to-day recognition systems that we and other companies have used successfully for a number of years.

Perhaps you want to start from scratch and introduce a complete recognition system in your company or organization. Or if you have some elements already in place, you may need to implement only one or two additional dimensions and the specific processes associated with them. Maybe you have always used certain recognition techniques but you haven't identified them as such — which is often the case with informal group recognition.

> *Tell me — I'll forget.*
> *Show me — I may*
> *remember.*
> *Involve me — and I'll*
> *understand.*
>
> **Tennant**
> **philosophy/motto**

When it comes to recognition, each company has its own unique history, culture, and mode of operation. For that reason, the road to recognition for every organization is a journey of surprises, filled with challenges and opportunities. While every recommendation may not be appropriate for every organization, the three-dimensional model can be adapted to meet a variety of needs.

START WITH SELF-ASSESSMENT

To begin, size up your current situation. Where are you now? Where do you want to be?

Before you develop a comprehensive recognition plan, you must determine your organization's recognition readiness and practice. At Tennant, we've developed a brief assessment to help organizations take the first step toward evaluating their company's recognition style. Circle the letter that generally represents your organization:

Management Understanding and Attitude

1. Overall Attitude
   a. Little thought is given to recognition.
   b. Awareness grows; some recognition programs are in place.
   c. Recognition is a regular and continuous activity.

2. Recognition's Place in Company Culture
   a. No systematic approach exists.
   b. Recognition is seen as an important element of motivation.
   c. Recognition system is an essential part of company culture.

3. Frequency
   a. Recognition is sporadic.
   b. Frequency is built into existing systems.
   c. Refined feedback systems allow highest level of frequency possible.

4. Recognition Responsibilities
   a. No accountability; everyone thinks it's someone else's job.
   b. A few individuals are "recognition crusaders."
   c. All of management is involved; some are genuine champions.

5. Whose Job is Recognition?
   a. Management believes it's personnel's job.
   b. Responsibility shifts to department managers.
   c. Recognition is **everybody's** job.
6. Awareness that Employees Need Recognition
   a. Management thinks, "That's what they get paid for."
   b. Awareness dawns: "Maybe people DO like recognition."
   c. "IF people like recognition, AND people are important, THEN recognition is important."

Kinds/Methods of Recognition

7. a. Traditional: Rewards for safety, service, sales; salary increases.
   b. Additional kinds are added to the traditional.
   c. A variety of kinds/methods are used to fit varied values.

Percentage of Total Employee Population Recognized

8. a. Limited.
   b. Increased numbers.
   c. ALL.

Training

9. a. No specific recognition training is done.
   b. Efforts are focused in managerial/supervisory training and on the different kinds and techniques of recognition.
   c. Entire population is trained in specific techniques and the importance of recognition.

Follow-Up and Improvement Actions

10. a. None.
    b. Some short-range efforts are made.
    c. Recognition is included in long-range planning. Continual activity with a feedback system is in place.

Measurement

11. a. Traditional means: Quantitative only (number of grievances, employee turnover, etc.).
  b. Employee values and perceptions are surveyed and tracked.
  c. Survey results are used to tailor efforts to meet employee needs.

Financial

12. a. "Recognition costs too much."
  b. Management realizes that investment is needed.
  c. Management believes that investment in recognition will yield a 10-fold return in employee satisfaction.

After answering the questions above, tally your score to determine where your organization stands in regard to recognition:

1. Count the number of "a" answers and fill in the number here: _____

2. Count the number of "b" answers, multiply that number by 2, and put that total here: _____

3. Count the number of "c" responses and multiply that number by 3. Put the total here: _____

4. Add the sub-totals for the grand total. _____

What the scores mean:

If your organization scores 12 to 19 points, it can be described as a **traditional** organization. If you fall into the 20 to 27 point range, your organization is **transitional**. Finally, if you score between 28 and 36 points, your organization can be described as **visionary** (see chart at right). Now let's take a look at these terms and what they signify.

How Your Organization Scores

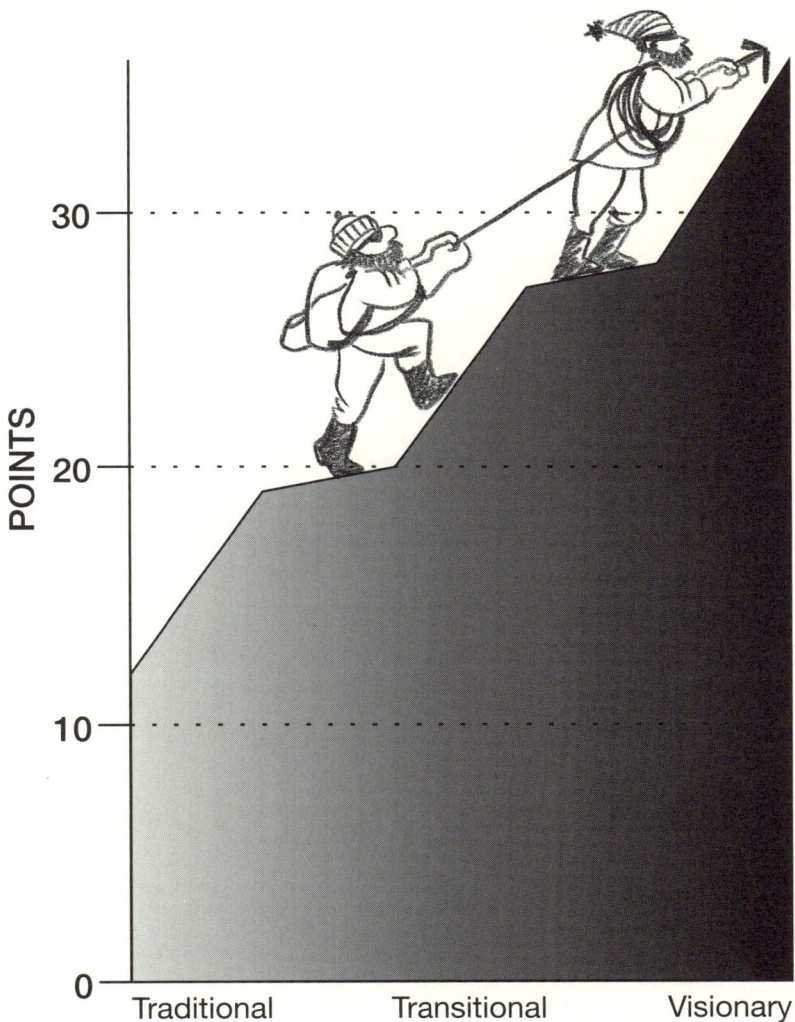

POINTS

30 ·······

20 ·······

10 ·······

0

Traditional   Transitional   Visionary

TRADITIONAL

Traditional organizations are largely unaware of the importance of recognition. They operate under the assumption that a paycheck is thanks enough for a good job. They may believe that recognition is an added expense that drains financial resources instead of improving the bottom line. Or they are satisfied with current levels of performance and profitability and feel that things are fine as they are. Though many traditional organizations may appear to operate effectively, if they neglect or ignore recognition, they are missing an opportunity to improve quality, efficiency, and productivity and create a more satisfying work environment for their employees.

TRANSITIONAL

Organizations that score between 20 and 27 points on the assessment are well on their way to achieving quality recognition. In these companies, recognition practices are probably becoming the norm rather than the exception. Even day-to-day verbal feedback, the most difficult recognition dimension to master, is becoming more frequent and more comfortable. Although there is room for improvement in these organizations, recognition is definitely headed in the right direction.

VISIONARY

Visionary organizations have attained a level of performance that far exceeds most other companies. They are reaping the rewards of long-term commitment to recognition in a number of ways — high morale, low turnover and absenteeism, higher productivity, and increased efficiency. They have also created an upbeat and positive work atmosphere that people thoroughly enjoy. To those within this point range — congratulations! You deserve some recognition for this achievement. Keep up your evolutionary process.

THE EVOLUTION OF RECOGNITION — ACHIEVING EXCELLENCE

If you examine closely the previous self-assessment, you will see that the move from traditional to transitional and finally to visionary status is an evolutionary process. Even with the best intentions and maximum effort, it won't happen overnight.

In Chapter 1, we outlined the four key elements to a successful recognition program — management commitment; employee involvement; cooperation; and time, energy, and determination. Now that we've recounted our recognition story, it is probably evident that these elements are basic, broad, and interrelated.

To achieve recognition excellence requires a commitment to all these principles and a willingness to withstand critical self-examination and numerous missteps. Progress comes from learning the most from your experiences and constantly adapting and refining your approach to achieve maximum results. It's a long journey, but it's a satisfying one. Consider the following factors as you proceed.

MANAGEMENT RESPONSIBILITIES

What do you want to accomplish? Higher productivity? Improved safety? Better customer service? All of these objectives can be better met through effective recognition. But while a commitment to the concept of recognition is commendable, successful recognition requires in-depth management analysis and planning on three levels.

First, management must acquire thorough knowledge and understanding of the organization, including its culture and its current status. In other words, "who we are and how we do business." Second, management must identify the organization's recognition objectives — in specific terms where it wants to go. Bridging the gap between the current status and these objectives requires a comprehensive strategy. This means outlining the specific standards of performance and identifying the behaviors that lead to it. Third, these performance guidelines must be linked to overall company goals.

Benchmarking is an effective way to determine objectives. By examining the performance of other organizations, a company can set its sights on achievable goals and develop strategies for getting there.

ESTABLISHING A BASELINE ASSESSMENT

Nothing gives you a clearer picture of where you're going than seeing where you've been. For that reason, we strongly recommend making a baseline assessment before tackling a major recognition effort. A baseline measurement is a barometer of current employee perceptions, attitudes, problems, and issues the organization must confront to implement recognition effectively. Baseline information can be gathered through employee surveys, focus group discussions, or management-driven evaluations. Some steps to take:

- establish the gap between current and desired performance;
- help determine the first steps and set priorities;
- provide a means to plot progress;
- identify problems;
- create an awareness of what needs to be accomplished; and
- help define what constitutes "good" recognition.

According to the Minnesota Council on Quality, once a baseline has been established, it should be monitored every two to three years to track changes and results. To do this correctly, an organization must duplicate the original survey — ask the same questions in the same way as it did the first time. This will give an accurate account of change.

EMPLOYEE INVOLVEMENT

Developing three-dimensional recognition requires the participation of people throughout the organization — not just management. This means involving employees in planning and implementation. The more involvement the better. This will ultimately save time by pinpointing employee problems, issues, and perspectives. It will also help determine how to set goals, monitor progress, and keep the process on track.

> *"People know the company, they want to do a good job, and they are willing to solve problems. Promoting their involvement is one way to improve their satisfaction and feeling of belonging."*
>
> **Paul Brunelle**

Employee involvement in the recognition process has two other advantages: it enhances program credibility and it promotes program value and significance. When starting from scratch, why eliminate the largest source of creative input? Recognition is most successful as a team effort in which everyone partakes.

As we discussed in Chapter 4, involvement in itself is a type of recognition. People want to participate, and those given the opportunity find it deeply satisfying. In a 1991 *Training* magazine report on rewards and recognition, the writer stated, "Employee participation in the planning process increases the chances that a program will be accepted as fair and that prizes or rewards will reflect workers' tastes."[1]

At Tennant, we offer a number of opportunities to encourage employee involvement, ranging from organized cross-functional problem-solving groups to Patent Awards, which provide recognition and encouragement for employee innovation.

TRAINING AND SKILL-BUILDING

Management must be committed not only to the concept of recognition, but to its practice. This calls for in-depth training on the importance of recognition, the different types necessary to meet diverse employee needs, and training and skill-building to deliver it consistently and properly.

Training and skill-building throughout an organization increase participation and involvement, keep the momentum going, keep awareness high, and ensure that recognition is properly given and received.

Training also provides valuable on-the-job skills as well. In a 1991 study, Learning International, Stamford, Connecticut, identified six well-developed competency areas found in superior customer-contact employees. Four of the six areas were related to listening and communication skills.

As we have mentioned, early in Tennant's quality process we offered a specific course on communication called Listening and a course on team building, Working Together©. A third course, Group Process Skills®, focused on understanding group dynamics and improving the effectiveness of group efforts in meeting company goals. Most Tennant employees have attained these skills, so the need for the first two courses has declined. However, we still offer classes on communication skill-building, conducting effective meetings, three-dimensional recognition, and group problem solving.

Like other types of involvement, training and skill-building contribute to improved cooperation among employees at all levels. With information and knowledge comes understanding. Being "in the loop" helps dispel suspicion and resistance to change. Teaching people how to listen and respond in a clear, non-critical way improves relationships. It puts everyone on the same team — which is essential for an organization trying to reshape its culture.

ACCOUNTABILITY

To succeed, every recognition process must include guidelines for accountability. At Tennant, that accountability has sifted down through the organization over the years. It began as a management-sponsored effort and later included all supervisors. Today, every Tennant employee is responsible for recognizing others. Performance in that area is evaluated every year during the employee's annual review.

TIME, ENERGY, AND DETERMINATION

As we mentioned in Chapter 1, time, energy, and determination are essential if a company wants to change. A review of the previous chapters of this book reveals that building a solid recognition system at Tennant was hard work. It has been more than a decade since we began our Quality Improvement efforts, of which recognition is an important part, and we are still building, improving, and refining it. Meeting the diverse needs of our employees is an ongoing process. We owe it to ourselves and the company to maintain the level of excellence we have achieved. And that takes work.

THREE-DIMENSIONAL RECOGNITION

A review of each dimension of Tennant's recognition program — formal, informal, and day-to-day — shows that each is unique. And each fulfills a unique employee need. The charts shown on the following pages provide a graphic example of this simple truth:

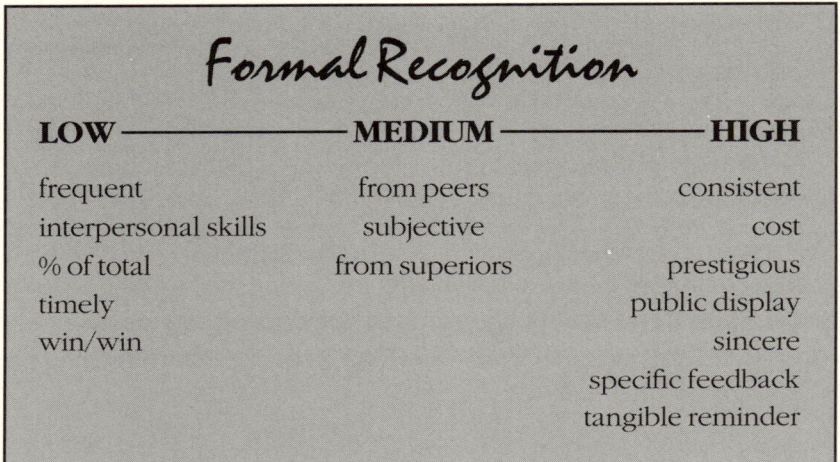

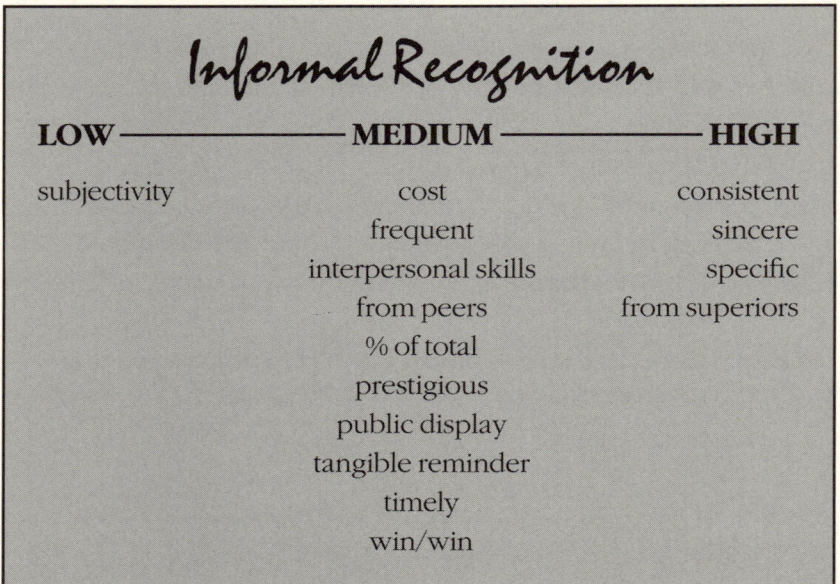

Formal Recognition

LOW	MEDIUM	HIGH
frequent	from peers	consistent
interpersonal skills	subjective	cost
% of total	from superiors	prestigious
timely		public display
win/win		sincere
		specific feedback
		tangible reminder

Informal Recognition

LOW	MEDIUM	HIGH
subjectivity	cost	consistent
	frequent	sincere
	interpersonal skills	specific
	from peers	from superiors
	% of total	
	prestigious	
	public display	
	tangible reminder	
	timely	
	win/win	

Day-to-Day Recognition

LOW —————— **MEDIUM** —————— **HIGH**

cost	consistent
prestigious	frequent
public display	interpersonal skills
subjective	from peers
tangible reminder	% of total
	sincere
	specific feedback
	from superiors
	timely
	win/win

Three-dimensional recognition offers options that can be planned, budgeted, implemented, and tracked. With commitment and consistency, three-dimensional recognition, in its various forms, can reach every corner of your organization to create an integrated, cohesive work force that is productive, involved — and happy to be part of the team.

Whether it's extended by individuals or organizations, recognition directly acknowledges employees' contributions to an organization's goals, large and small. In the process, it bolsters employee self-esteem — that source of confidence and inner strength everyone needs to achieve top performance. A commitment to recognition is an ongoing investment in an organization's most valuable resource — its people. It is also an investment that costs little or nothing while generating enormous returns — decreased turnover and absenteeism, and increased productivity, pride, and job satisfaction. Quite simply, recognition puts everyone on the same team reaching for the same goal — success.

Kayser-Roth Corporation

When Kayser-Roth Corporation, manufac-turer of No-Nonsense Pantyhose, decided to implement Total Quality, the company started from the ground up. Rather than jumping into the fray with a boilerplate program, the Greensboro, North Carolina-based company polled a sample of its 6,500 "teammates" to mark the company's starting point. Employee teammates contributed their perceptions of total quality, assessed the company's existing recognition policies, and identified pertinent issues regarding teammate recognition. Responses were used to identify recognition opportunities that would be both meaningful and fair. They also provided a base-line measurement that could be used later to assess change and the impact of particular recog-nition programs.

"Initially we found we weren't doing a very good job of recognizing teammates," says Jane Martin, Kayser-Roth's vice president of Total Quality Management. She says the company had been doing some informal recognition and positive feedback, but the process was not systematic or comprehensive (there were no formal programs in place). Using the baseline survey as a guide, the company created formal recognition guidelines that gave the company divisions leeway to design and implement their own programs. "We like to let people grow their own gardens, within broad company parameters," says Martin. "In creating the plan, everyone came to a real understanding of how important recognition is to the quality process."

A year after recognition was formally instituted, Kayser-Roth did a follow-up survey to measure program success and employee change. The results showed substantial improvement. Clearly, laying the groundwork through baseline measurement has given Kayser-Roth a clear direction in its quality and recognition journey.

Gathering Information from a Focus Group

Focus groups can help organizations gather information essential to the planning and implementation of a successful recognition process. Not only can they help identify the types of recognition employees value, they can help identify how and when recognition should be given. You might use the following questions to start things off:

1. What kind of recognition, appreciation, or reward have you received from your work? How did you feel about it?

2. What kinds of recognition, appreciation, and rewards would you like to have in ABC Company? (List as many as possible.) From whom do you want this?

3. How do you know that your work is worthwhile, valuable, or appreciated? (Ask yourselves what events, actions, or situations are most likely to make you feel that way.)

4. What should the organization (your company or division) reward or recognize? For example, hard work, going above and beyond the call of duty, teamwork, etc.

5. Some people believe that individual awards make sense; some believe having a group

singled out is best. What do you think? Rewards and recognition can occur for individuals or for groups; what do you think ABC Company or your division should do?

6. If ABC Company were to create a special process for awards, who should these come from: peers? a committee? your manager? How might a reward or recognition system work? Should there be a nominating process; who should nominate; who should select; how should they be announced?

7. What can individual supervisors do to provide rewards or recognition? What have you seen supervisors do that is effective? How could supervisors do this better?

8. Help us brainstorm. If ABC Company creates non-monetary rewards for special efforts or results, what kinds of non-monetary rewards could these be? Gifts, days off, plaques, conference attendance?[2]

❖

Acknowledgments

Most book acknowledgments are probably overlooked by the vast majority of readers — especially since the intent is to provide a personal note of appreciation from the authors to people who helped make the book possible. This objective is particularly noteworthy because of the subject of this book — recognition — and the desire to recognize everyone who had a part in bringing *Recognition Redefined* from ideas and concepts to the printed page.

So it is particularly important to offer heartfelt thanks to the many individuals who directly contributed to *Recognition Redefined*. There are many additional contributors beyond these mentioned, but the following gave not only their time, counsel, and expertise, but extended these contributions to that which borders on heart, blood, and soul.

Credit for the co-creation of the three-dimensional concept on which this book is based goes to Tennant's John Davis and Burt Thulin. The various Recognition Committee members quoted within these pages certainly bear mentioning as well as those who went before them and those who will follow. Internal company expertise was also offered by Paul Brunelle, Louise Quast, Doreen Larson, Jeff Fliss, Linda Deml, Bruce Borgerding, and Iris Staubus.

Production support has certainly been another key factor. Transforming concepts into final product has been expertly executed by contributing writer Mame Osteen, graphic designer Rachel Fine, and illustrator Jackie Urbanovic.

Trust, respect, patience, persistence, and friendship are only a few terms possible to describe project director Bonnie Anderson's input. Always there; always with an answer; always willing to help; always with an eagle eye; always organized; and always right! Her sparkle and effervescence have bubbled and proved contagious throughout these months.

Six years have transpired since *Quest for Quality* was published with Susan Mundale's direction. Her strength, diplomacy, and vision have also guided us in this project.

More directly involved has been Tennant's Quality Services staff — small in numbers but big in talent and heart. Since late 1989, Denise Parks has helped spread the recognition message through not only her on-the-job efforts, but by the ways she lives as well. Never have I met someone more inclined to err on the side of looking at the positive and expecting the best. In 1991, we were joined by Rick Radomsky. He has grounded us with his perspective and tackled multi-dimensional projects effortlessly. It's through his candor and commitment to quality we've been able to further spread Tennant's concepts.

Finally, to those people I can never thank enough for their lifelong support. Every life is a continual shaping process founded in early values. Deep appreciation goes to my parents, Fergy and Marie, for their support, confidence, and love. Seven years my junior, my brother Marty has re-emerged as a friend and confidant. As we've matured and our lives have become more parallel, we've been able to reconnect on similar wavelengths.

And of course, there's my partner and friend, Kevin, who proves that through marriage, we can complement our counterparts. Logical versus emotional would be one of the many pairs of antonyms one could use to describe us, but thankfully it works, and will spill into our next decades together. And also because of Kevin, there's Krista — the greatest joy of my life. I look forward to watching her grow and develop self-esteem as presented through the concepts of this book.

The nurturing environment at Tennant, created by Roger L. Hale, is the source for the words contained within these pages. I only hope others may learn and grow from it as I have.

Rita F. Maehling
July 1992

Notes

Chapter 1

1. McGraw-Hill, 1979.
2. Kenneth Blanchard, Ph.D., "Communication Skills Crucial for the '90s," *Quality Digest*, Apr. 1991.
3. Nathaniel Branden, *Honoring the Self: The Psychology of Confidence and Respect*, Bantam Books, 1983.
4. John Vasconcellos, quoted in *Minneapolis Star Tribune*, "Self-esteem is healthy for society," Nov. 27, 1990.
5. Janis Allen with Gail Snyder, *I Saw What You Did & I Know Who You Are*, Performance Management Publications, 1990.
6. Roger Hale, *Quest for Quality*, Tennant Company, 1987.
7. Blanchard, "Communication Skills Crucial for the '90s."
8. "Group Process Skills for Work Teams®," TrainingWorks Corporation. "Working Together: Improving Communications on the Job," © 1980, Interpersonal Communications Programs, Inc., Sherod Miller, Daniel B. Wackman, Dallas R. Demmitt, Nancy J. Demmitt.
9. Blanchard, "Communication Skills Crucial for the '90s."
10. Donald L. McLaurin and Shareen Bell, in "Open Communication Lines Before Attempting Total Quality," *Quality Progress*, June 1991.
11. Craig Miller, "Motivating Middle Managers," *Reward & Recognition*, supplement to *Training*, Aug./Sep. 1991.
12. Source: *Industry Week*.

Chapter 2

1. Bob Davis and Dana Milbank, "If the U.S. Work Ethic is Fading, Laziness May Not be the Reason," *Wall Street Journal*, Feb. 7, 1992.
2. Debra Kent, "Beyond 30something," *Working Woman*, Sep. 1990.
3. Mike Meyers, "Survey of workers finds it's not such a material world," *Minneapolis Star Tribune*, Jan. 11, 1989.
4. Linda DeStefano and Andrew Kohut, "People who identify with jobs found to be happier," *Minneapolis Star Tribune*, Sep. 5, 1989.
5. Kent, "Beyond 30something."

6. Linda DeStefano and Andrew Kohut, "People want more than just pay from their jobs," *Minneapolis Star Tribune*, Sep. 4, 1989.
7. Marc Hequet, "Non-Sales Incentive Programs Inspire Service Heroes," *Reward & Recognition*, supplement to *Training*, Aug. 1990.
8. Ibid.
9. DeStefano and Kohut, "People who identify with jobs found to be happier," *Minneapolis Star Tribune*, Sep. 5, 1989.
10. Ron Zemke, "Workplace Stress Revisited," *Training*, Nov. 1991.
11. Janis Allen, *I Saw What You Did*.
12. Katherine Ann Samon, "The Brash Pack: How to Manage the Twenty-Something Generation," *Working Woman*, Aug. 1990.
13. Craig Miller, "How to Construct Programs for Teams," *Reward & Recognition*, supplement to *Training*, Aug./Sep. 1991.
14. Source: *Industry Week*.
15. Alan Zimmerman, "Problems from a Lack of Recognition," The Zimmerman Communi•Care Network, © 1989.
16. John H. Sheridan, editor, "Memos," *Industry Week*, Nov. 21, 1988.
17. "The Under-Appreciated Quit," *Performance Management Magazine*, Vol. 7, No. 4. Credited to Sanford Teller Communications, Apr. 1989.

Chapter 3

1. From an unpublished manuscript, Cynthia Olson and Nancy Branton, "Motivating Your Employees." Based, in part, on D. Hellriegel, J. W. Slocum, Jr., and R. W. Woodman, *Organizational Behavior*, 5th edition, West Publishing Company, 1989.
2. Kenneth A. Kovach, "What Motivates Employees? Workers and Supervisors Give Different Answers," *Business Horizons*, Sep./Oct. 1987.
3. Ibid.
4. Ibid.
5. Sirota, Alper & Phau, New York, Telephone Survey 1989.
6. M.R. Cooper, B.S. Morgan, P. M. Foley and L. B. Kaplan, "Changing Employee Values: Deepening Discontent?" *Harvard Business Review*, Volume 57, 1979.
7. Marilyn B. Gilbert/Thomas F. Gilbert, "What Skinner Gave Us," *Training*, Sep. 1991.
8. Aubrey C. Daniels and Theodore A. Rosen, Ph.D., co-authors, *Performance Management: Improving Quality and Productivity Through Positive Reinforcement*, 3rd edition, revised, Performance Management Publications, 1989.

9. Gallup Organization, Inc., for Accountants on Call, a temporary employment agency, 1989. Cited in "Surprise! Workers Like Their Jobs," *Training*, March 1989.

CHAPTER 4

1. Hequet, "Non-Sales Incentive Programs."
2. Ibid.
3. Source: Gail Snyder, "Tangible Reinforcers: The Good, The Bad, and The Ugly," *Performance Management Magazine*, Vol. 8, No. 1.
4. Philip C. Grant, Ph.D., "Rewards: The Pizzazz is in the Packages, Not the Prize," *Personnel Journal*, March 1988.
5. Blanchard, "Be Creative When You're Rewarding Employees," *Quality Digest*, Dec. 1991.
6. Kenneth Blanchard, Ph.D., and Spencer Johnson, M.D., co-authors, *The One Minute Manager*, William Morrow and Company, 1982.
7. Blanchard, "It pays to praise," *Today's Office*.

CHAPTER 6

1. Cited in "What Rewards Work?" *Reward & Recognition*, supplement to *Training*, Sep. 1991.
2. Pat Samples, "In Non-Sales Setting, Quick Rewards Work," *Reward & Recognition*, supplement to *Training*, Aug. 1990.
3. *In Search of Excellence*, Harper & Row, 1982.
4. "The best new managers will listen, support, motivate," Sep. 1990.
5. Blanchard, *The Blanchard Management Report*.
6. Source: Manu Vora, member of Technical Staff, ISCBU, and Belinda Brandon, Quality Manager, SSBU.

CHAPTER 7

1. Aubrey C. Daniels and Theodore A. Rosen, Ph.D., Performance Management Publications, 1989.
2. Ibid.
3. Susan Feyder, "Secretaries don't always want what managers think they do," *Minneapolis Star Tribune*, Apr. 14, 1992.
4. N. Branton, T. Olson, and S. Wickham, "Minnesota Department of Natural Resources Career Paths Study," May 1987.
5. Samples, "In Non-Sales Setting, Quick Rewards Work."
6. Kathryn Wall & Rosalind Jeffries, "Changing Values Change Rewards," *Reward & Recognition*, supplement to *Training*, Aug. 1990.

7. Blanchard, *The One Minute Manager*.
8. Allen, op. cit.
9. McLaurin & Bell, "Open Communication Lines Before Attempting Total Quality."
10. Blanchard, "Communication Skills Crucial for the '90s."

CHAPTER 8

1. Paul Nolan, "Selling Recognition Programs Up, Down & All Around," *Reward & Recognition*, supplement to *Training*, Sep. 1991.
2. Source: "Rewards and Recogniton at the MN Dept. of Natural Resources," 1990, Nancy Branton.

Index

More Tennant Quality Books from Monochrome Press

Discover how this manufacturer of floor maintenance equipment and products has evolved during the last decade through quality improvement.

In each of the following books from Tennant's library, you'll learn how you can put successful quality-improving procedures, ideas, and techniques to work in your organization.

Made in the USA: Strategic Supplier Quality Management

Made in the USA tells you how you can have strong purchasing leadership, improve supplier quality, and develop better relationships with your suppliers.

With a foreword by Tom Peters, Tennant executives Roger L. Hale, Ronald E. Kowal, Donald D. Carlton, and Tim K. Sehnert detail seven critical success factors to improve your supplier quality. These are proven techniques used every day by Tennant. *Made in the USA* will show you how you can use these techniques to develop an integrated supplier/manufacturer relationship that will give your customers better quality than your competition.

Quest for Quality

Among other things, *Quest for Quality* gives you a chronicle of Tennant's 12-year quality-improvement journey. In this book, you'll get an inside look at everything from Tennant's very first steps into quality, to the successful programs and practices used today.

With a foreword by Tom Peters and introduction by Phil Crosby, Tennant executives Roger L. Hale, Douglas R. Hoelscher, and Ronald E. Kowal outline the five key elements of a successful quality program. They also offer specific tools managers can use to inspire total quality within your own organization.

For more information about these books and others, contact Gray Media, Inc., P.O. Box 424, Exeter, New Hampshire 03833, (800) 497-3060 or (603) 778-9212.